HARCOURT

Math

Harcourt

Orlando   Austin   Chicago   New York   Toronto   London   San Diego

Visit *The Learning Site!*
www.harcourtschool.com

For permission to reprint copyrighted material, grateful acknowledgment is made to the following sources:

Barefoot Books Ltd.: Cover illustration by Debbie Harter from *Bear in a Square* by Stella Blackstone. Illustration copyright © 1998 by Debbie Harter.

Charlesbridge Publishing: Cover illustration by Frank Mazzola, Jr. from *The Crayon Counting Book* by Pam Muñoz Ryan and Jerry Pallotta. Illustration copyright © 1996 by Frank Mazzola, Jr.

Childrens Press: Cover illustration from *Math Counts: Pattern* by Henry Pluckrose. © 1994 by Watts Books. Published by Childrens Press®, 1995.

Greenwillow Books, a division of William Morrow & Company, Inc.: Cover illustration by Jose Aruego and Ariane Dewey from *One Duck, Another Duck* by Charlotte Pomerantz. Illustration copyright © 1984 by Jose Aruego and Ariane Dewey.

Harcourt, Inc.: Cover illustration by Maria Majewska from *Ten Little Mice* by Joyce Dunbar. Illustration copyright © 1990 by Maria Majewska. Cover illustration from *Sea Shapes* by Suse MacDonald. Copyright © 1994 by Suse MacDonald. Cover illustration from *One Potato: A Counting Book of Potato Prints* by Diana Pomeroy. Copyright © 1996 by Diana Pomeroy.

HarperCollins Publishers: Cover photograph from *Exactly the Opposite* by Tana Hoban. Copyright © 1990 by Tana Hoban. Cover illustration by Felicia Bond from *The Right Number of Elephants* by Jeff Sheppard. Illustration copyright © 1990 by Felicia Bond.

Margaret K. McElderry Books, Simon & Schuster Children's Publishing Division: Cover illustration by Keiko Narahashi from *What's what?* by Mary Serfozo. Illustration copyright © 1996 by Keiko Narahashi.

The Millbrook Press.: Cover illustration from *Bears at the Beach: Counting 10 to 20* by Niki Yektai. Copyright © 1996 by Niki Yektai.

Random House Children's Books, a division of Random House, Inc.: Cover illustration by Bob Barner from *Benny's Pennies* by Pat Brisson. Illustration copyright © 1993 by Bob Barner. Cover illustration by Jose Aruego and Ariane Dewey from *Five Little Ducks* by Raffi. Illustration copyright © 1989 by Jose Aruego and Ariane Dewey.

Troll Communications L. L. C.: Cover illustration by Cheryl Nathan from *The Long and Short of It* by Cheryl Nathan and Lisa McCourt. Illustration copyright © 1998 by Cheryl Nathan.

Printed in the United States of America

ISBN 0-15-352221-6

6 7 8 9 10 030 10 09 08

© Harcourt

Senior Author

Evan M. Maletsky
Professor of Mathematics
Montclair State University
Upper Montclair, New Jersey

Authors

Angela Giglio Andrews
Math Teacher, Scott School
Naperville District #203
Naperville, Illinois

Jennie M. Bennett
Houston Independent School District
Houston, Texas

Grace M. Burton
Professor, Watson School of Education
University of North Carolina at Wilmington
Wilmington, North Carolina

Lynda A. Luckie
K–12 Mathematics Coordinator
Gwinnett County Public Schools
Lawrenceville, Georgia

Joyce C. McLeod
Visiting Professor
Rollins College
Winter Park, Florida

Vicki Newman
Classroom Teacher
McGaugh Elementary School
Los Alamitos Unified School District
Seal Beach, California

Tom Roby
Associate Professor of Mathematics
California State University
Hayward, California

Janet K. Scheer
Executive Director
Create A Vision
Foster City, California

Program Consultants and Specialists

Janet S. Abbott
Mathematics Consultant
California

Elsie Babcock
*Director, Mathematics and Science
Center*
Mathematics Consultant
Wayne Regional Educational Service
Agency
Wayne, Michigan

William J. Driscoll
Professor of Mathematics
Department of Mathematical Sciences
Central Connecticut State University
New Britain, Connecticut

Lois Harrison-Jones
Education and Management Consultant
Dallas, Texas

Rebecca Valbuena
*Language Development
Specialist*
Stanton Elementary School
Glendora, California

Contents

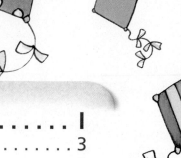

© Harcourt

iv

Unit 2

CHAPTER 3

Theme: A Nature Adventure

NUMBERS 0 to 5 55

© Harcourt

v

© Harcourt

Unit 3

CHAPTER
6

Theme:
Fun on
the Farm

NUMBERS 10 to 30 135

© Harcourt

Unit 5

CHAPTER 9

Theme:
Vegetable
Garden

MEASUREMENT 215

Unit 5

CHAPTER 10

Theme:
My
Kindergarten
Classroom

Unit 6

CHAPTER 11

Theme:
Springtime
All Around

© Harcourt

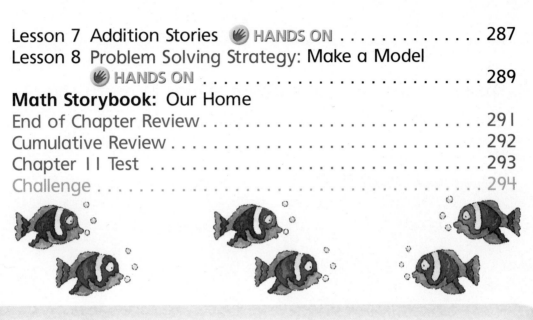

Unit 6

CHAPTER **12**

Theme:
Here
Comes
Summer

SUBTRACTION 295

Why Learn Math?

You will learn lots of exciting things in math this year that you can use in your everyday life.

Sort and Classify

HARCOURT **Math**

HARCOURT

Circle the objects that look like the object in the middle.

Photography Credits:

All photography by Harcourt photographers listed, © Harcourt: Weronica Ankarorn, Victoria Bowen, Ken Kinzie, Sheri O'Neal, Quebecor Imaging, and Terry Sinclair.

Ilustration Credits:

Linda Bild: Storybook; **Michelle Noiset:** 1, 2; **Richard Holding:** 5, 6, 7; **Susan Hall:** 8, 9, 13, 14; **Jane Yamada:** 10, 19, 20, 21, 22; **Daniel DelValle:** 11, 12; **Nancy Freeman:** 17; **Mary Thelen:** 23.

SCHOOL HOME CONNECTION

Dear Family,
    Today we started Chapter 1, Sort and Classify. We will learn about positions, such as over and under and left and right. We will also learn to sort objects that are alike in some way.

    Love,

_____

Vocabulary Power

left   **right**

sort (to put into groups) These shapes can be sorted by their color.

group (a set or a collection) These shapes are all alike in color. They make a group.

ACTIVITY

- Invite your child to help you sort the laundry. Ask your child to tell how the clothes in each pile are alike. (*They are all white towels.*) Then ask what word(s) can be used to name each pile (*dark clothes, jeans*).

BOOKS TO SHARE

To read about sorting and classifying with your child, look for these books at your local library.

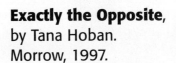

Exactly the Opposite, by Tana Hoban. Morrow, 1997.

How Many Snails? by Paul Giganti, Jr. Morrow, 1994.

Is It Red? Is It Yellow? Is It Blue? by Tana Hoban. Morrow, 1987.

Visit *The Learning Site* for additional ideas and activities. www.harcourtschool.com

© Harcourt

3

MATERIALS: a different kind of small object, such as buttons, pennies, or paper clips, for each player

DIRECTIONS: Play with a partner and decide who goes first. Each player takes a turn placing one object in a space. To win, a player must have three of his or her objects going across, down, or diagonally and say in what way they are alike.

Name _____

Circle the top block.
Circle the bottom clown.
Circle the middle hat as you go from top to bottom.

Use red to color the flowerpot in the top window. Use yellow to color the flowerpot in the middle window. Use blue to color the flowerpot in the bottom window.

 HOME ACTIVITY • Ask your child to show you the *top, middle,* and *bottom* shelves of a bookcase, closet, or cabinet.

 Circle the bird that is in the cage.
Circle the fish that is out of the bowl.
 Circle the car that is out of the box.
Circle the bear that is in the balloon.

Draw a car in the sandbox. Draw a truck out
of the sandbox.

HOME ACTIVITY • Lay a piece of yarn in a
circle on the floor. Have your child tell you when
he or she is in the circle or out of the circle.

8

Name _____

Circle the rabbit that is above the table. Mark an X on the rabbit that is below the table.

Circle the object that is over the boat. Mark an X on the object that is under the boat.

© Harcourt

9

Circle the bird that is over the sand castle. Circle the crab that is under the sand castle. Circle the shell that is below the bridge.

© Harcourt

HOME ACTIVITY • Have your child point to objects that are *above, below, over,* and *under* things in your home.

10

Name _____

 **Left**

Right

Draw green apples on the tree on the left.
Draw red apples on the tree on the right.

 **Left**

Right

 Use red to circle the car on the right.

Use green to circle the building on the left.

 Use red to circle the tree on the right.

HOME ACTIVITY • Have your child describe the pictures, using the words *left* and *right*.

12

Problem Solving Skill
Use a Picture

Circle the butterfly that is over the clown
suit. Circle the pair of shoes on the left.
Look at the shelf with hats. Circle the hat
in the middle.

PROBLEM SOLVING

13

Color the top balloon. Color the bird that is below the other bird. Color the gift that is on the right. Color the clown that is out of the hoop.

🏠 **HOME ACTIVITY** • Have your child draw an outline of a house. Tell him or her to add a chimney on top, windows in the middle, and a tree to the left of the house.

14

Name _____

✅ Review

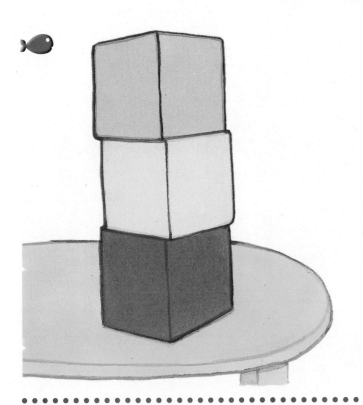

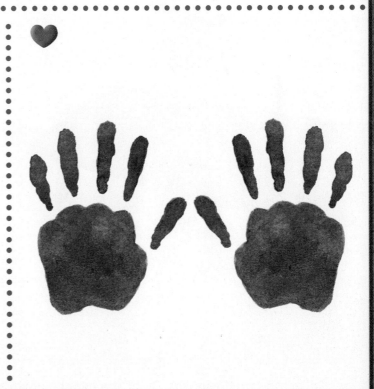

🐟 Circle the top block and mark an X on the bottom block.
🐢 Circle the fish that is in the fishbowl.
⭐ Circle the bird that is over the tree.
❤ Circle the right hand and mark an X on the left hand.

✔ Cumulative Review

🐟 Color the top clown red. Color the middle clown blue.
Color the bottom clown yellow.
🐢 Circle the bird that is out of the bird cage.
⭐ Circle the butterfly that is above the table.
Mark an X on the butterfly that is below the table.
❤ Color the tree on the left green. Color the tree on the right red.

🐟 🐢 ⭐ ♥ Sort the shoes by color. Mark an X
on the one that is not like the others.

◯ Circle

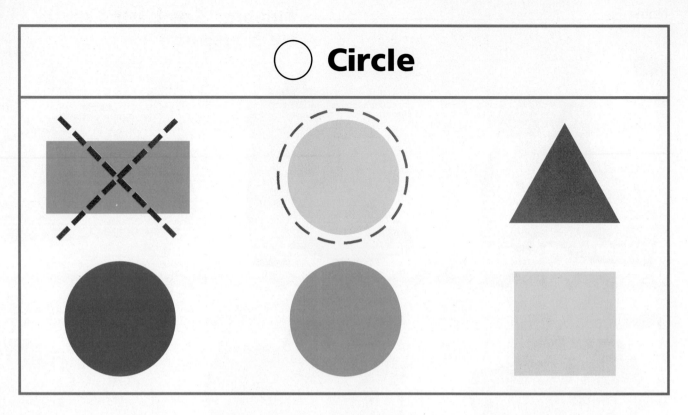

△ Triangle

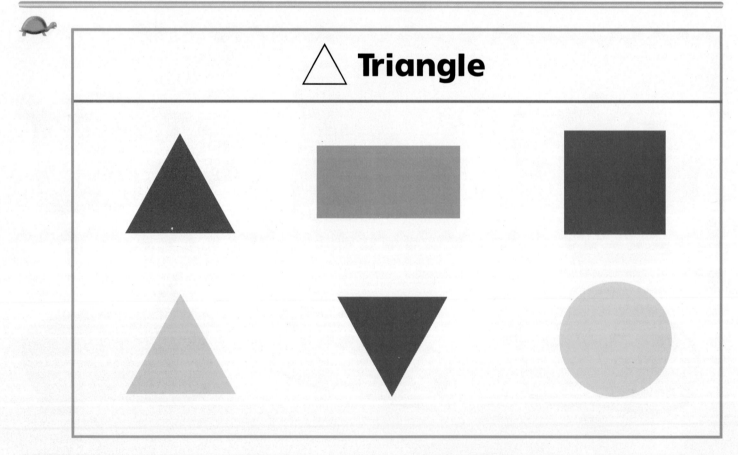

Circle the shapes that belong in the group.
Mark an X on the shapes that do not belong.

⬟ **HOME ACTIVITY** • Mix up three pairs of socks
of different solid colors. Ask your child
to sort the socks by color.

Name _____

Algebra: **Sort by Size or Kind**

 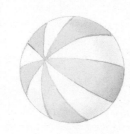  

  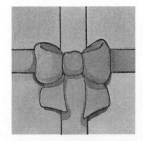

 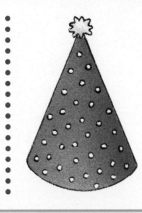    

Look at the ball at the beginning of the row. Circle the balls that are the same size.
Look at the kite at the beginning of the row. Circle the kites that are the same size.
Look at the gift at the beginning of the row. Circle the gifts that are the same size.
Look at the hat at the beginning of the row. Circle the hats that are the same size.

19

Sort the shirts by kind.
Draw each shirt on the clothesline that has shirts of the same kind.

HOME ACTIVITY • Help your child sort his or her shirts by kind.

20

Name _____

Make a
Concrete Graph

HANDS ON

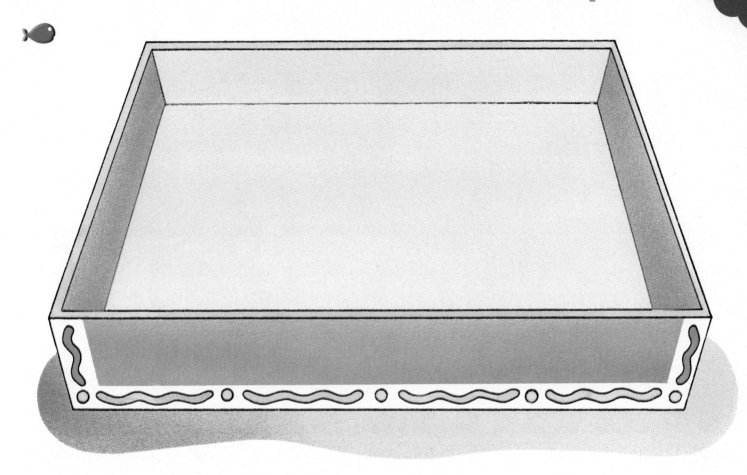

Red and Blue Cubes

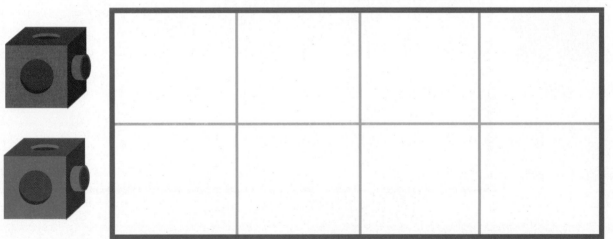

━━━━━━━━━━━━━━━━━━━━━━━━━━━━━━━━━

Place a handful of connecting cubes in the box.
Sort your cubes by color.
Move your red cubes to the top row on the graph.
Move your blue cubes to the bottom row on the graph.
What does this graph tell you about the cubes?

© Harcourt

21

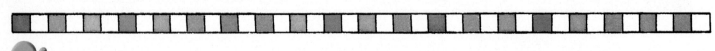

Large and Small Bears

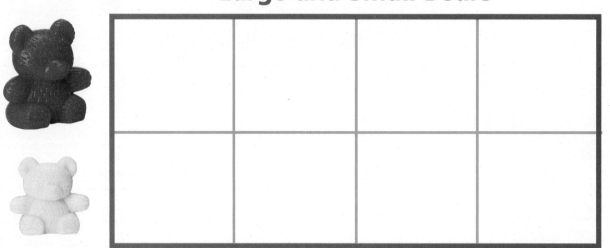

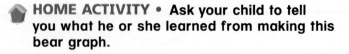 Place a handful of bear counters in the box. Sort your bear counters by size.

 Move your large bear counters to the top row on the graph. Move your small bear counters to the bottom row on the graph. What does this graph tell you about the bear counters?

HOME ACTIVITY • Ask your child to tell you what he or she learned from making this bear graph.

Problem Solving Strategy
Use Logical Reasoning

Three of the objects are alike. Which object does not belong with the others? Mark an X on it, and tell why.

   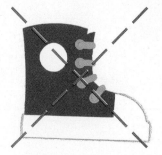

    Three of the objects are alike. Which object does not belong with the others? Mark an X on it, and tell why.

HOME ACTIVITY • Help your child sort his or her toys by shape. Ask why certain toys do not belong in each group.

Party Colors and Shapes

By _____

HOME ACTIVITY • This book will help review positions and sorting. Invite your child to share this book with you.

© Harcourt

Which shape is on the right?

3

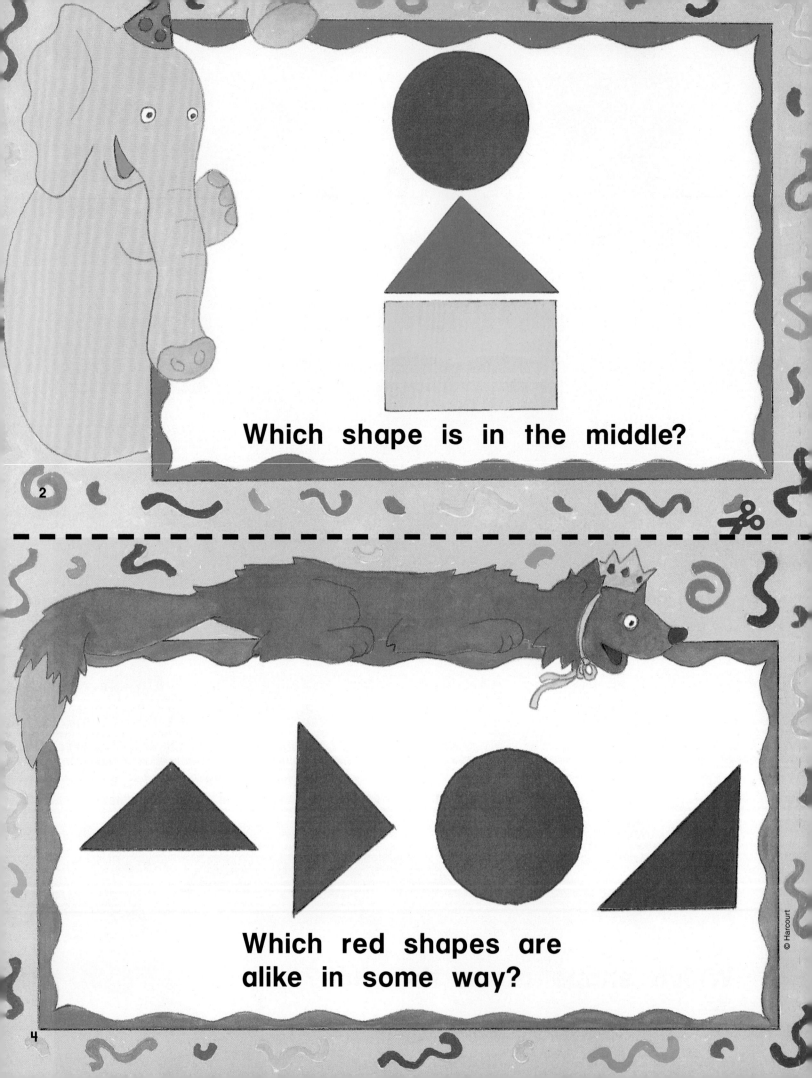

Which shape is in the middle?

2

Which red shapes are alike in some way?

4

Where does this △ triangle belong?

5

Which present does not belong?

7

How are the two shapes
in each group alike?

6

Draw two shapes that are
alike in some way.

8

© Harcourt

Name _____

✅ Review

   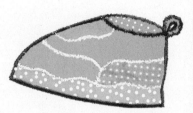

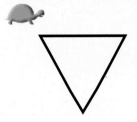    

 Sort the shoes by color. Mark an X on the shoe that is not like the others.

 Look at the shape at the beginning of the row. Circle the shapes that are the same. Mark an X on the shapes that do not belong.

 Look at the gift at the beginning of the row. Circle the gifts that are the same size.

 Look at the flower at the beginning of the row. Circle the flowers that are the same kind.

 Mark an X on the object that does not belong.

25

✔ Cumulative Review

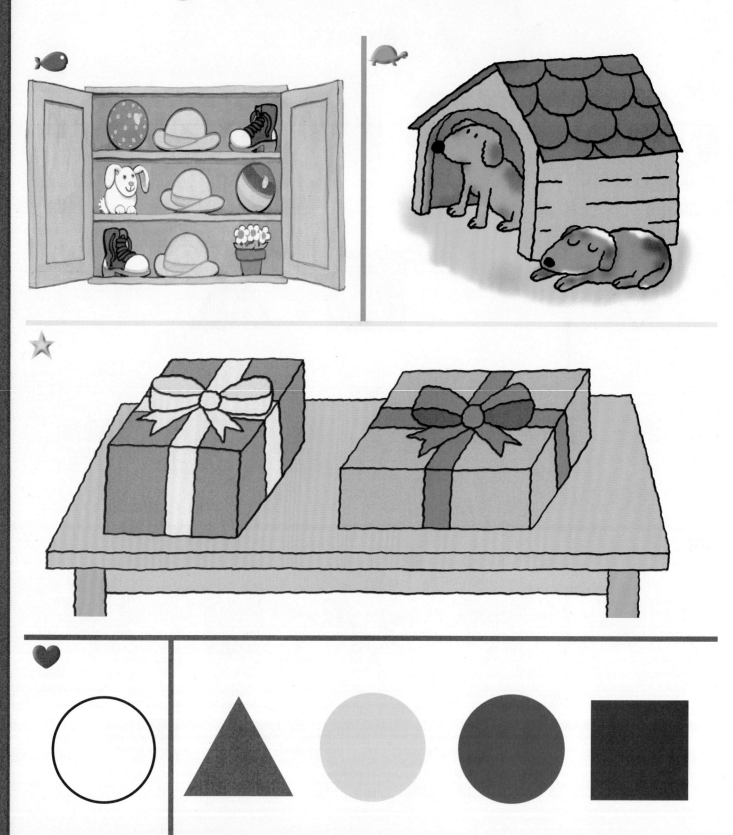

🐟 Circle the middle hat as you go from top to bottom.
🐢 Circle the dog that is out of the doghouse.
⭐ Circle the gift on the left and mark an X on the gift on the right.
❤ Look at the shape at the beginning of the row. Circle the shapes
that are the same. Mark an X on the shapes that do not belong.

Name _____

✅ Test

 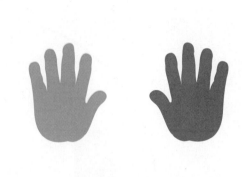

   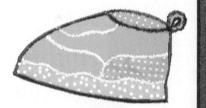

CHAPTER 1 • TEST

Circle the object below the bridge.
Circle the hand on the right.
Look at the hat at the beginning of the row. Circle the hats that are the same size.
Sort the shoes by color. Mark an X on the shoe that is not like the others.
Mark an X on the object that does not belong.

27

CHALLENGE
Alike in Color and Shape

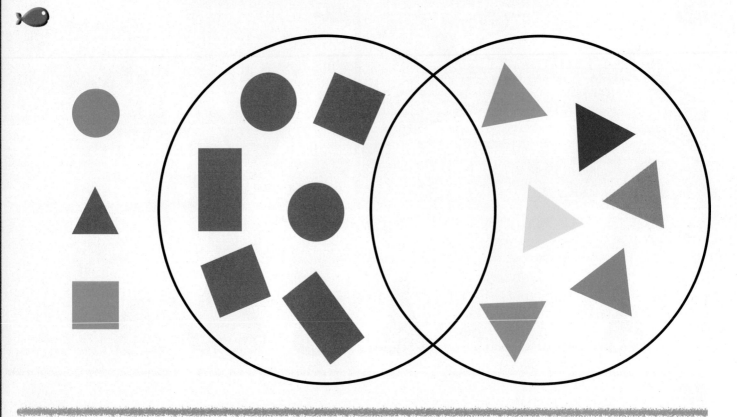

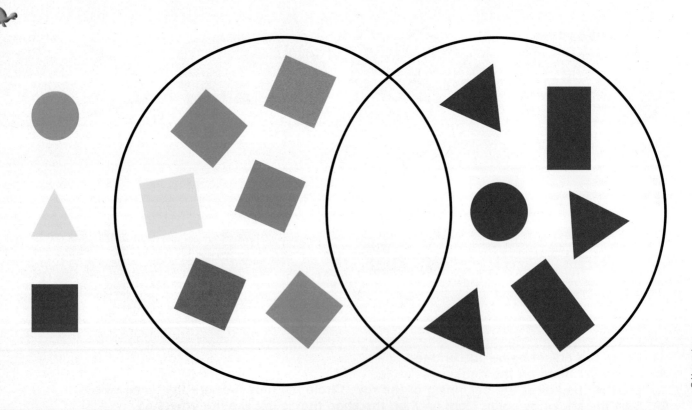

Draw the shape that belongs in both groups. Tell why.

Patterns

 Circle the two objects that are alike.

Photography Credits:
All photography by Harcourt photographers listed, © Harcourt: Veronica Ankarorn, Victoria Bowen, Ken Kinzie, Sheri O'Neal, Quebecor Imaging, and Terry Sinclair.

Illustration Credits:
Joe Boddy: 51, 52 storybook; **Deborah Borgo:** 31, 41, 42; **Shelley Dieterichs:** 33, 34, 43; **Nancy Freeman:** 44; **Patrick Girouard:** 32; **Heidi King:** 52; **Dan McGeehan:** 47, 48; **Jill Meyerhoff:** 39, 40, 45, 46; **Mary Thelen:** cover.

© Harcourt

SCHOOL HOME CONNECTION

Dear Family,

Today we started a new chapter, Patterns. We will copy patterns, show what comes next in patterns, and make new ones. We will also find the part of a pattern that repeats again and again.

Love,

_____

Vocabulary Power

patterns

- Help your child discover patterns in wallpaper, clothing, or dishes. Look for patterns outdoors together as well.

BOOKS TO SHARE

To read about patterns with your child, look for these books in your local library.

Math Counts: Pattern, by Henry Pluckrose. Children's Press, 1995.

One, Two, Three, Jump! by Penelope Lively. Simon and Schuster, 1999.

© Harcourt

31

Math Game

The repeating part of the pattern is ⬤ ◻. Help the
squirrel follow the ⬤ ◻ pattern path to its acorns.

32

Act out the pattern. Say the pattern as you act
out each part. Circle what you would most likely do next.

🐟 🐟 ⭐ Act out the pattern. Say the pattern as you act out each part. Circle what you would most likely do next.

⬟ HOME ACTIVITY • Invite your child to show you a sound or action pattern. Copy your child's pattern.

34

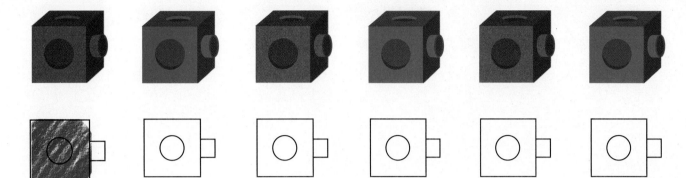

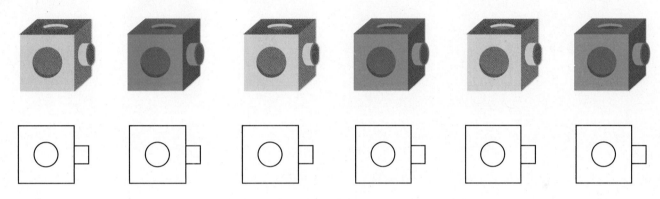

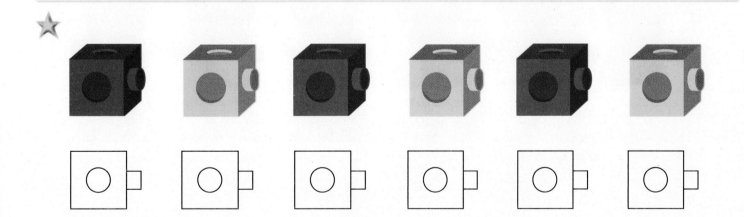

Put cubes on the pattern. Read the pattern.
Color the cubes to copy the pattern.

35

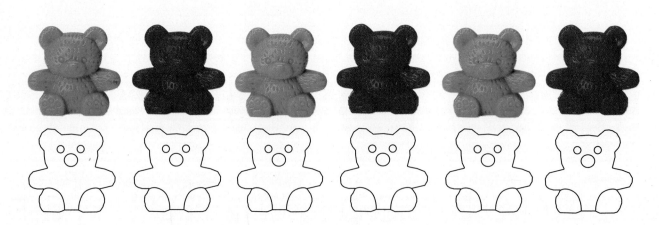

Read the pattern. Color the bear counters to copy the pattern.

HOME ACTIVITY • Help your child find patterns in buildings, wallpaper, or fabrics. Have your child draw the patterns he or she finds.

36

© Harcourt

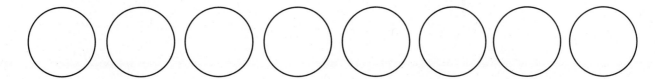

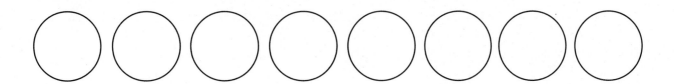

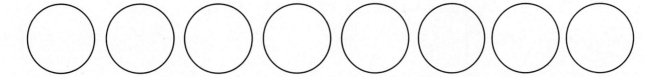

Color the counters to copy the pattern and show what most likely comes next.

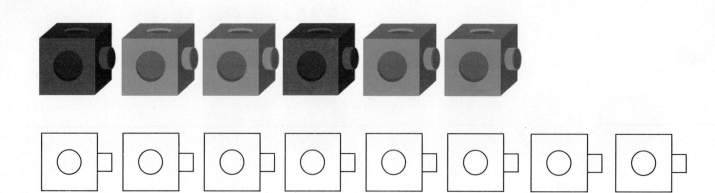

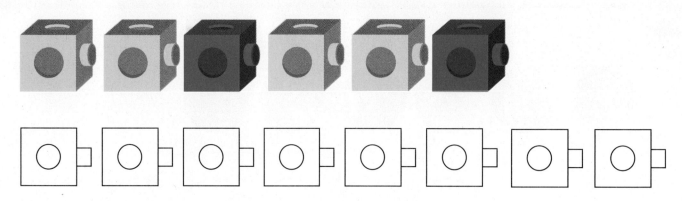

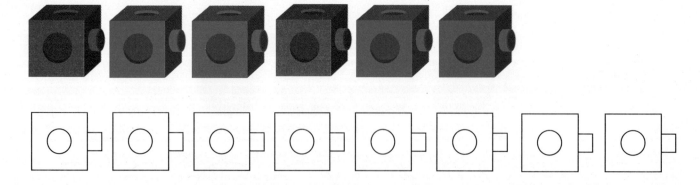

Color the cubes to copy the pattern and show what most likely comes next.

HOME ACTIVITY • Have your child sort pasta pieces by color and/or shape, arrange them in a pattern, and then string them to make a necklace.

Algebra: **Predict and Extend Patterns**

    What color cubes do you think come next? Color the cubes to show what most likely comes next.

🐟 🐢 What color counters do you think come next? Color to show what most likely comes next.
⭐ 🖤 What color cubes do you think come next? Color to show what most likely comes next.

🏠 **HOME ACTIVITY** • Help your child use simple objects to make a pattern.

40

Name _____

Problem Solving Skill
Transfer a Pattern

PROBLEM SOLVING

© Harcourt

Use bear counters or act out to show the same pattern. Draw the pattern.

41

Use counters or act out to show the same pattern. Draw the pattern.

HOME ACTIVITY • Have your child use different objects to show one of the patterns on this page.

42

Name _____

✔ Review

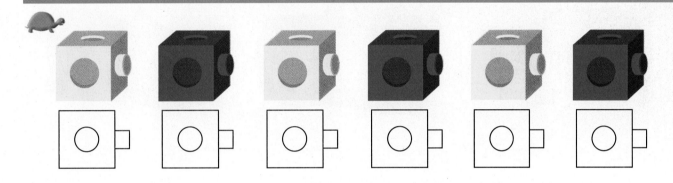

 Circle what you would most likely do next.

🐢 Color the cubes to copy the pattern.

⭐ Color the counters to copy the pattern and show what most likely comes next.

❤ Color to show what most likely comes next.

✅ Cumulative Review

 Circle the tree on the right.

 Sort the shoes by color. Mark an X on the shoe that is not like the others.

 Color the bears to copy the pattern.

💜 Color to show what most likely comes next.

44

Name _____ Algebra:
Understand a Pattern

Read the pattern. Circle the part that repeats
again and again.

45

Read the pattern. Circle the part that repeats again and again.

HOME ACTIVITY • Make a simple pattern. Invite your child to read it and tell which part repeats again and again.

46

Name _____

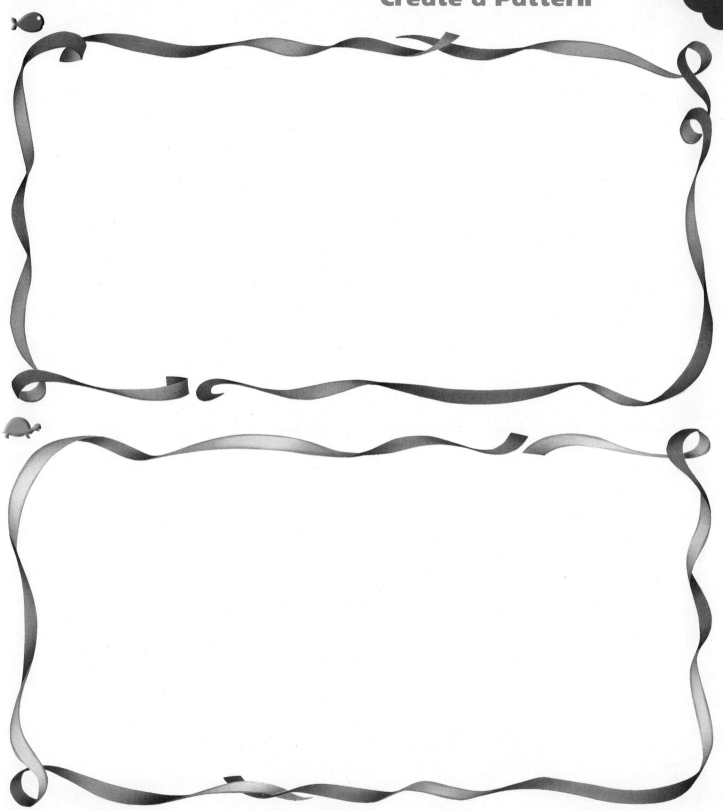

Use counters to make your own pattern. Draw your pattern.

Use large and small bear counters to make your own pattern. Draw your pattern.

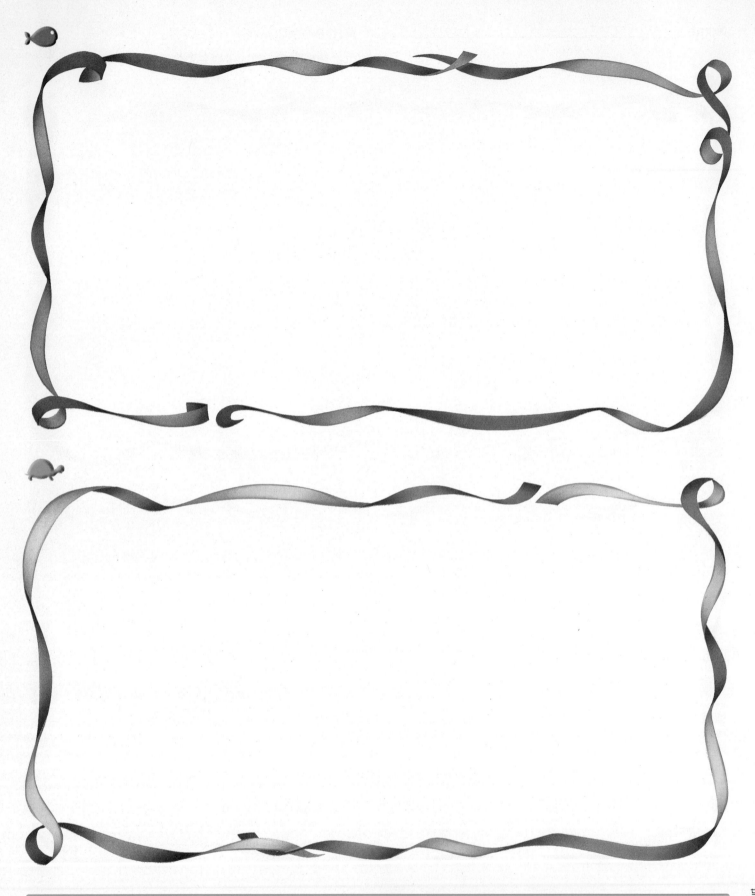

Use pattern blocks to make your own pattern. Draw your pattern.

Use crayons to make your own pattern. Draw your pattern.

HOME ACTIVITY • Have your child create a pattern with his or her toys. Ask your child to tell which part repeats again and again.

Name _____

Problem Solving Skill
Use a Pattern

 Read the pattern. Tell what part repeats again and again. Draw and color the missing shape in the pattern.

PROBLEM SOLVING

© Harcourt

49

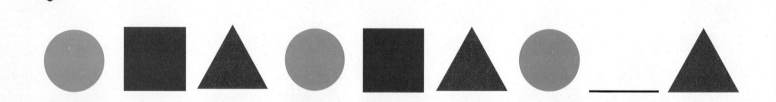

Read the pattern. Tell what part repeats again and again. Draw and color the missing shape in the pattern.

HOME ACTIVITY • Arrange objects in a pattern. Remove one object from the pattern. Have your child tell you the missing object and place it to complete the pattern.

© Harcourt

What Pattern Do You See?

By _____

🏠 **HOME ACTIVITY** • This book will help review patterns. Invite your child to share this book with you.

1

© Harcourt

What pattern do you see?
Color to copy the pattern.

3

What pattern do you see?
Talk about it.

2

What pattern do you see?
Color the apples to copy
the pattern. Then show what
most likely comes next.

4

What pattern do you see?
Draw dots to show what
most likely comes next.

5

What pattern do you see?
Draw pumpkins to show
what most likely comes next.

7

What pattern do you see?
Use counters or act out
to show the same pattern.

6

Draw flowers to make your
own pattern. What pattern
do you see?

8

What pattern do you see? Draw and color the missing shape.

9

What pattern do you see? Read the pattern and tell a friend.

11

Make and draw your own pattern. What pattern do you see?

10

What patterns do you see?

12

Name _____

✅ **Review**

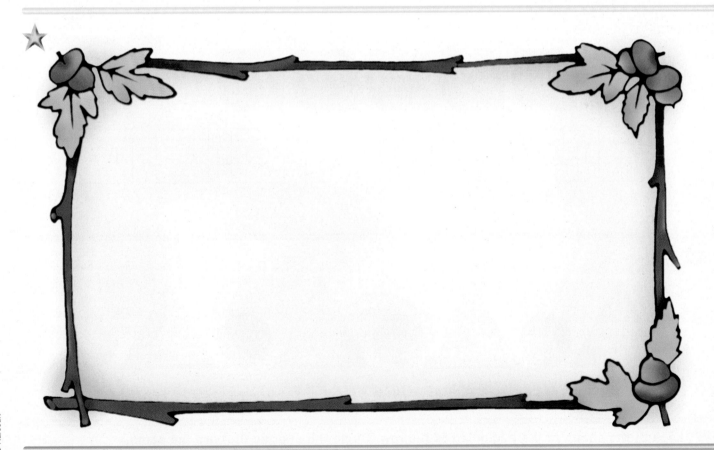

🐟 Circle the part of the pattern that repeats again and again.

🐢 Use bear counters or act out to show the same pattern. Draw the pattern.

⭐ Use connecting cubes to make your own pattern. Draw your pattern.

✅ Cumulative Review

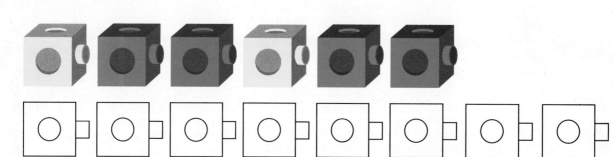

🐟 Look at the shape at the beginning of the row. Circle the shapes that are the same.
Mark an X on the shapes that do not belong.

🐢 Look at the flower at the beginning of the row. Circle the flowers that are the same kind.

⭐ Color the cubes to copy the pattern and show what most likely comes next.

♥ Circle the part that repeats again and again.

CHAPTER 2 • CUMULATIVE REVIEW

© Harcourt

52

Name _____

✓ Test

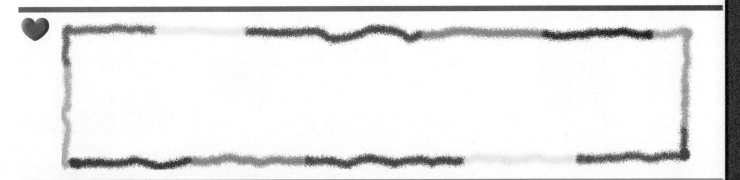

🐟 Color the bears to copy the pattern.

🐢 Color the cubes to show what most likely comes next.

⭐ Use bear counters to show the same pattern. Draw the pattern.

❤ Use cubes to make your own pattern. Draw your pattern.

CHALLENGE
Follow the Pattern

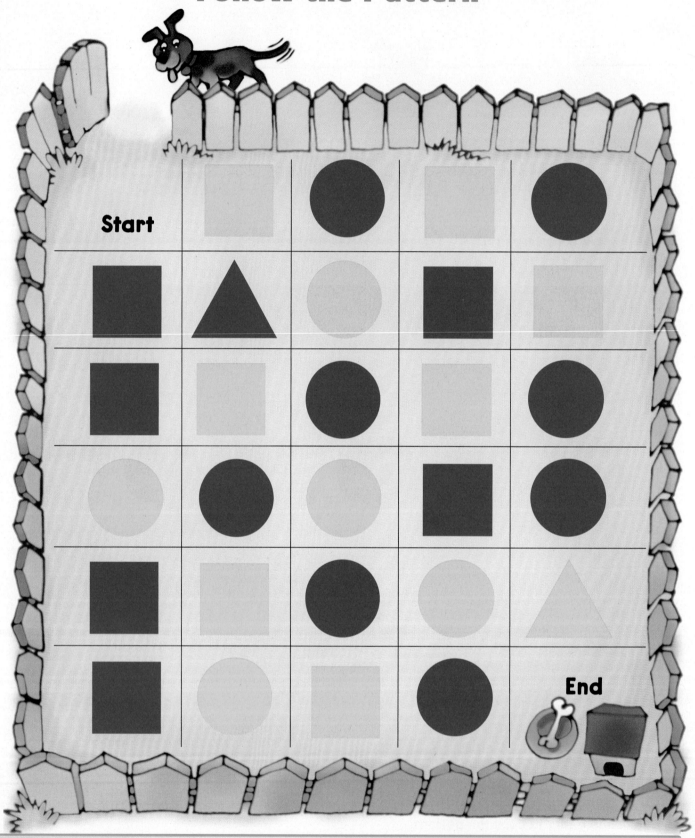

Start

End

Follow the ⬜ ● pattern to help the puppy find his home.
Draw a line to follow the pattern.

54

HARCOURT
Math

© Harcourt

Harcourt

Color to copy the pattern and show what most likely comes next.

Photography Credits:

All photography by Harcourt photographers listed, © Harcourt: Weronica Ankarorn, Victoria Bowen, Ken Kinzie, Sheri O'Neal, Quebecor Imaging, and Terry Sinclair.

Illustration Credits:

Ken Bowser: 62; **Sarah Dillard:** 71, 72; **Rusty Fletcher:** 77, 78; **Liisa Chauncy Guida:** 57; **Jennifer Beck Harris:** 69, 70; **Obadinah Heavner:** 65, 66; **Reggie Holliday:** 56; **Phyliss Horning:** cover; **Dave Klug:** 63, 64; **Benton Mahan:** 62, 75, 76; **Dan McGeehan:** 73, 74; **David Slonim:** storybook; **Steve Sullivan:** 62; **Deborah Tilley:** 61, 64; **Pamela Thomson:** 58; **Stan Tusan:** 59, 60.

© Harcourt

SCHOOL ⟷ HOME
C O N N E C T I O N

Dear Family,
  Today we started a new chapter, Numbers 0 to 5. We will learn how to match groups of objects. We will also learn to count objects, making sure that we have counted each one. We will study the numbers 0, 1, 2, 3, 4, and 5.

  Love,

_____

Vocabulary Power

more   fewer

There are more flowers than butterflies.
There are fewer butterflies than flowers.

same as   How many?

The number of frogs is the same as the number of lily pads.
How many frogs do I see? I see three.

Visit *The Learning Site* for additional ideas and activities. www.harcourtschool.com

A C T I V I T Y

- Invite your child to count with you.

- As you set the table, have your child match groups of items, such as forks and spoons, to see which groups have more, the same, or fewer.

BOOKS TO SHARE

To read books about counting with your child, look for these books in your local library.

One Duck, Another Duck, by Charlotte Pomerantz. Greenwillow, 1984.

Just Enough Carrots, by Stuart J. Murphy. HarperCollins, 1997.

Ten Black Dots, by Donald Crews. HarperCollins, 1986.

Math Game

Start

0

3

2

1

1

5

5

2

3

4

End

MATERIALS: small bag with 5 small objects (beans, buttons), a set of game markers (pennies, paper clips) for each partner

DIRECTIONS: Play with a partner and decide who goes first. Starting at zero, choose a path. Each player takes a turn grabbing a handful of items from the bag. The player counts the items, finds the matching number on his or her path, and places a marker on the number. The first player to have a marker on all of his or her lily pads wins.

58

Algebra: **Equal Groups**

Color one box for each animal.

🐟 Draw a ball of yarn for each cat.
🐢 Draw a stand for each bird.

Draw lines to match the objects in the two groups.
Compare the groups. Circle the group that has more.

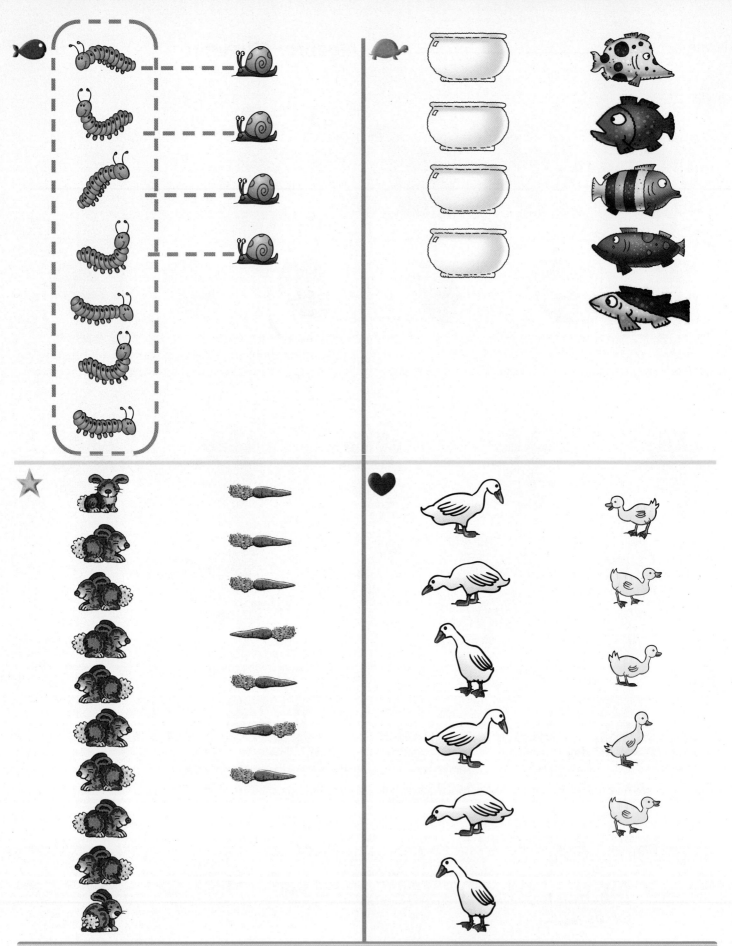

Draw lines to match the objects in the two groups. Compare the groups. Circle the group that has more.

HOME ACTIVITY • Ask your child to match the objects in two groups to find out which group has more.

62

© Harcourt

Draw lines to match the animals in the two groups.
Compare the groups. Circle the group that has fewer.

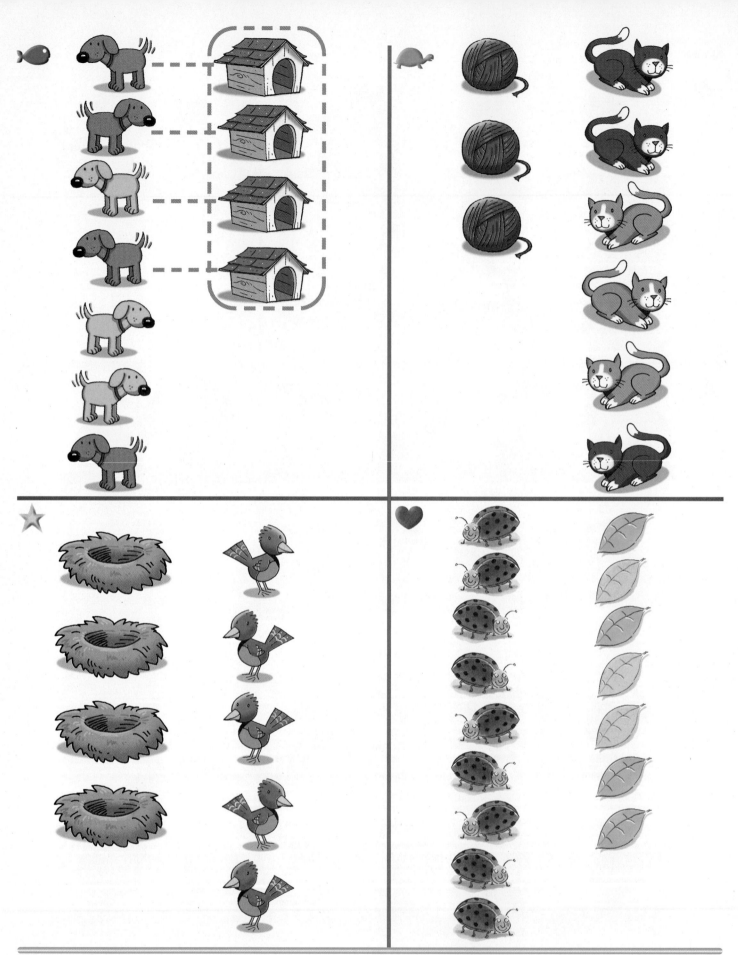

 © Harcourt

🐟 🐟 ⭐ ♥ Draw lines to match the objects in the two groups. Compare the groups. Circle the group that has fewer.

🏠 **HOME ACTIVITY** • Have your child match the objects in two groups to find out which group has fewer.

64

Name _____

Which Group Has More?

Put a handful of counters on the sunflower. Are
there more red counters or yellow counters? Move the
counters to the graph. Circle the group with more counters.

PROBLEM SOLVING

65

Which Group Has Fewer?

Put a handful of counters on the lily pad. Are there fewer red counters or yellow counters? Move the counters to the graph. Circle the group with fewer counters.

HOME ACTIVITY • Show your child a pile of two kinds of toys, such as blocks and balls. Have him or her make a graph by first lining up the blocks and then lining up the balls next to them. Ask your child which group has more.

Name _____

 Review

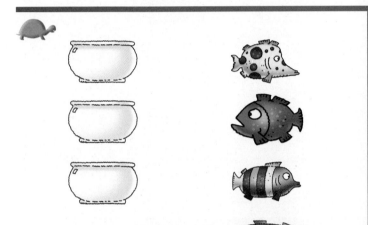  

 SHAPES

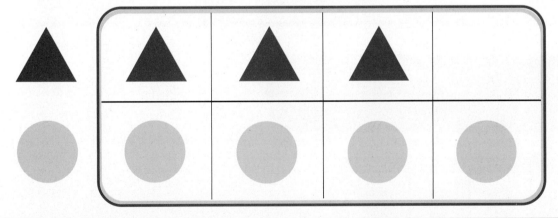

Draw a ball for each glove.
Draw lines to match the objects in the two groups.
Compare the groups. Circle the group that has more.
Draw lines to match the objects in the two groups.
Compare the groups. Circle the group that has fewer.
Circle the row on the graph with more shapes.

67

Cumulative Review

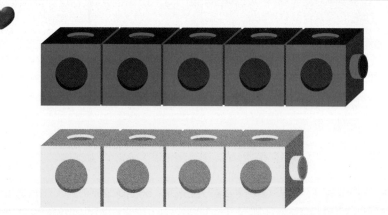

🐟 Circle the kites that are the same size.
🐢 Read the pattern. Color the cubes to copy the pattern.
⭐ Color the cubes to show what most likely comes next.
💜 Circle the group that has more.

Name _____

4
four

I
one

2
two

3
three

Look at the big picture. Use connecting cubes
to show how many. Draw the cubes. Trace the number.

69

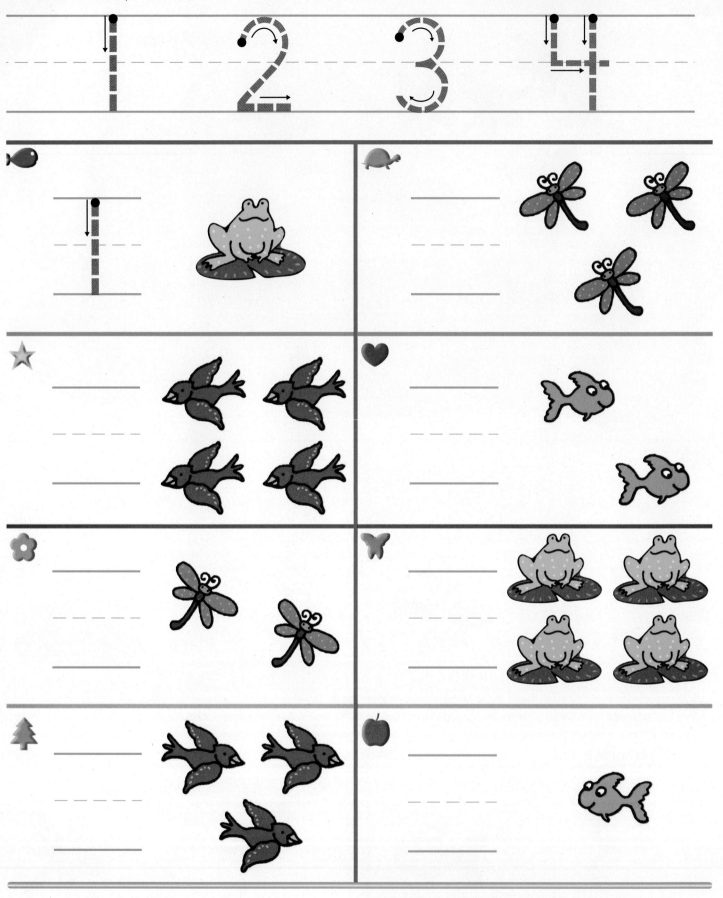

Count the animals in the group. Write the number.

HOME ACTIVITY • Draw two unequal groups of objects. Have your child match one penny to each object in each group. Which group has more? Which group has less?

70

Name _____

Five

5
five

Count the pinecones. Trace the number 5.
Circle the groups that have 5 pinecones.

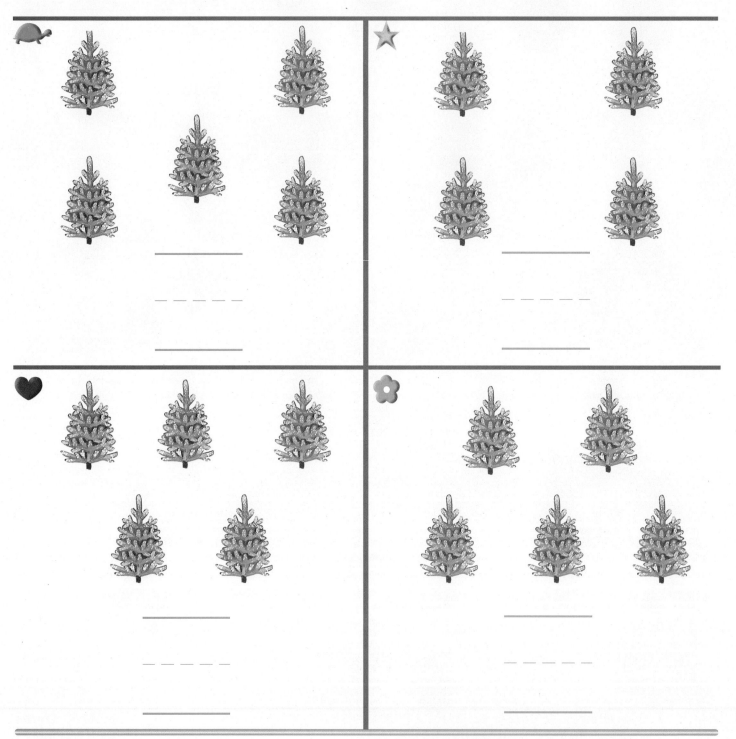

🐟 Trace the number 5.
🐢 ⭐ 💜 🌸 Count the trees. Write the number that tells how many.

🏠 HOME ACTIVITY • Have your child find groups of 5 objects at home, in stores, and around the neighborhood.

Name _____

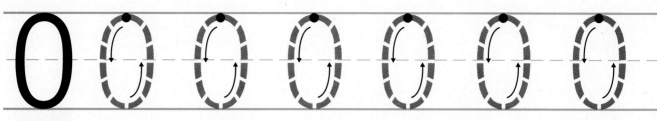

zero

© Harcourt

 Trace the number 0.

    Count the penguins. Write the number that tells how many.

How many 🐦?
0 (2)

How many 🐦?
0 4

How many 🐦?
0 3

How many 🐦?
0 5

🐟 🐟 ⭐ ❤ Count the puffins. Circle the number that tells how many. Then write the number.

HOME ACTIVITY • Hide 0, 1, and 2 buttons under three cups. Move the cups around and ask your child to find the one that has 0 buttons under it.

74

0 1 2 3 4 5

0 1 2 3 4 ___

___ 1 2 3 4 5

🐟 Write the number that is after 2.
🐢 Write the number that is after 4.
⭐ Write the number that is before 1.

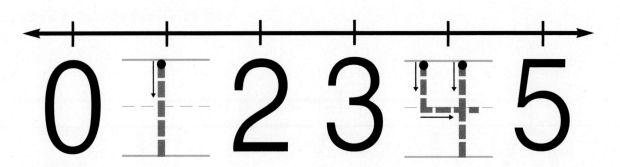

0 1 2 3 4 5

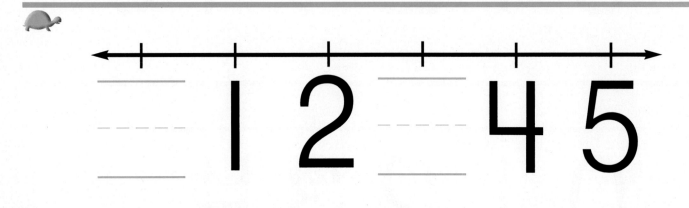

1 2 4 5

0 1 3 4

Write the number that is before 2.
Write the number that is after 3.
Write the number that is before 1.
Write the number that is after 2.
Write the number that is before 3.
Write the number that is after 4.

Name _____

PROBLEM SOLVING

Look at the card at the top of the page. It has 5 dots. Without counting, find cards with more than 5 dots. Circle the cards with more than 5 dots.

Look at the ladybug at the top of the page. It has 5 dots. Without counting, find ladybugs with fewer than 5 dots. Circle the ladybugs with fewer than 5 dots.

⬟ HOME ACTIVITY • Have your child place 5 dried beans in one jar and an unknown number in a matching jar for you to estimate how many. Then count together to find the exact number.

Birds

By _____

🔷 **HOME ACTIVITY** • This book will help review the numbers 0 to 5. Invite your child to share this book with you.

I can circle the group with more birds.

3

I can draw I
bird in each nest.

2

I can circle the group
with fewer birds.

4

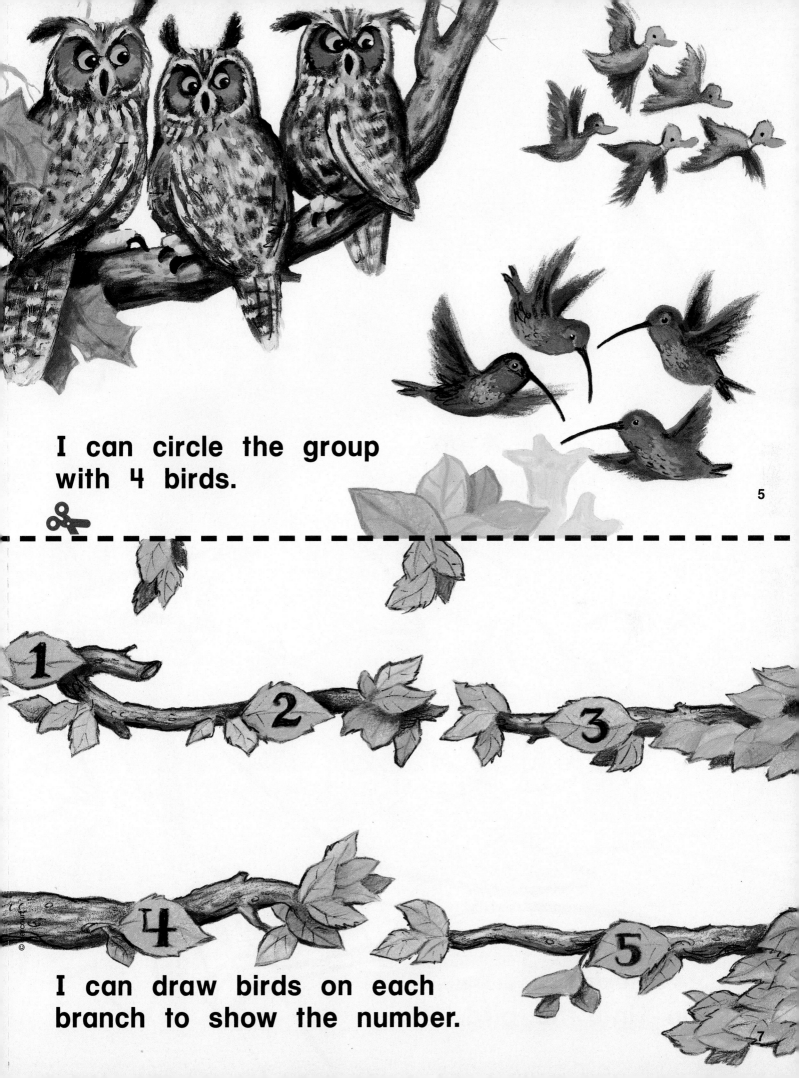

I can circle the group
with 4 birds.

5

I can draw birds on each
branch to show the number.

7

I can mark an X on
the nest with no birds.

6

I can find the bird.

8

© Harcourt

Name _____

★

_____

- - - - - - - -

_____

_____

- - - - - - - -

_____

_____

- - - - - - - -

_____

  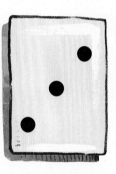  

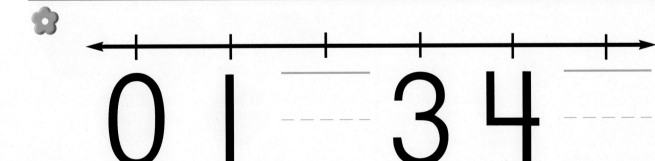

0 1 _ 3 4 _

🐟🐢⭐ **Count the objects in the group. Write the number.**
❤ **Look at the card with 5 dots. Without counting, circle the**
card with fewer than 5 dots.
🌸 **Write the number that is before 3. Write the number that is after 4.**

✅ Cumulative Review

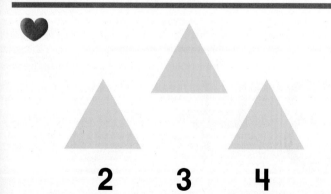

2 3 4

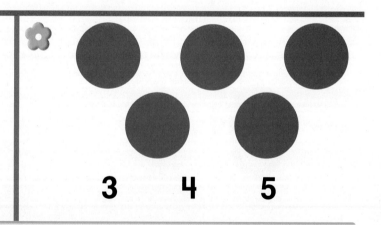

3 4 5

🐟 Mark an X on the object that does not belong.
🐢 Color to show what most likely comes next.
⭐ Use counters to show the same pattern. Draw the pattern.
❤🌸 Count the shapes. Circle the number that tells how many.

Name _____

✅ Test

0 ___ 2 3 ___ 5

 |

 **Circle the group that has more.**
Circle the group that has 5 pine cones.
⭐ **Write the number that is before 2. Write the number that is after 3.**
❤ **Look at the card with 5 dots. Without counting,**
circle the card with fewer than 5 dots.

 © Harcourt

CHALLENGE
Number Patterns

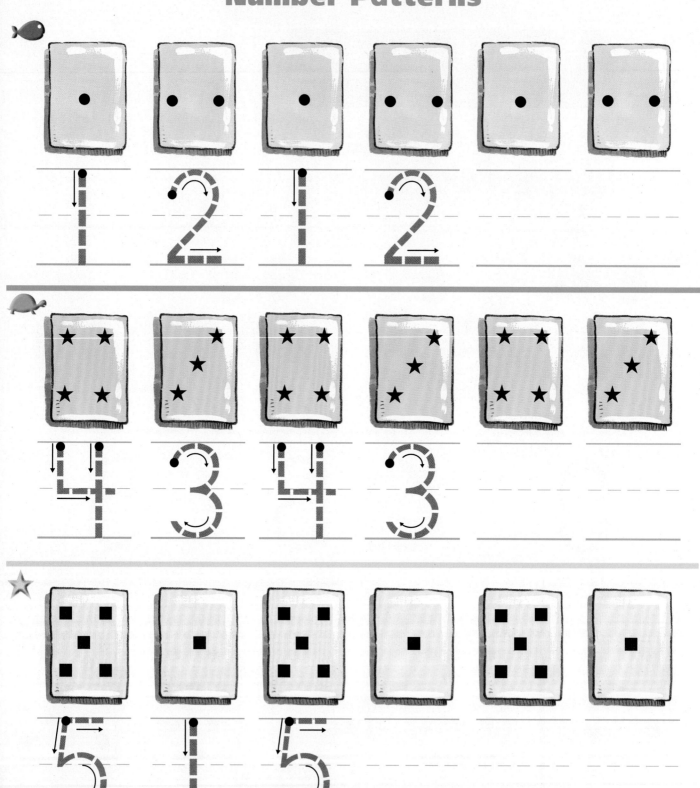

Look at the pattern.
Write the numbers that come next.

Numbers 6 to 10

Count the ants in each group.
Circle the groups that have the same number of ants.

Photography Credits:

All photography by Harcourt photographers listed, © Harcourt: Weronica Ankarorn, Victoria Bowen, Ken Kinzie, Sheri O'Neal, Quebecor Imaging, and Terry Sinclair.

Illustration Credits:

Ken Bowser: 91, 92; **Shirley Beckes:** 91, 92; **Roberta Collier-Morales:** 87, 89, 90; **Daniel DelValle:** 86; **Ben Mahan:** storybook; **John Nez:** 103, 104; **Rosiland Soloman:** cover, 83; **Ken Spengler:** 84; **Joe Veno:** 93, 94; **Jane Yamada:** 99, 100.

© Harcourt

SCHOOL HOME CONNECTION

Dear Family,

Today we started a new chapter, Numbers 6 to 10. We will match these numbers to groups of objects and learn which group has more than or less than another.

Love,

_____

Vocabulary Power

6 six

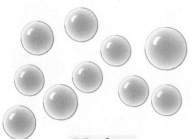

10 ten

ACTIVITY

- Have your child count groups of six, seven, eight, nine, and ten objects.

- Have your child compare two groups of objects. Ask him or her which group has more.

BOOKS TO SHARE

To read about numbers with your child, look for these books at your local library.

The Right Number of Elephants, by Jeff Sheppard. HarperCollins, 1990.

Who's Counting? by Nancy Tafuri. Greenwillow, 1986.

Barn Cat, by Carol P. Saul. Little Brown, 1998.

GO ON-LINE Visit *The Learning Site* for additional ideas and activities. www.harcourtschool.com

Math Game

MATERIALS: number cube (6–10), paper clips, buttons
DIRECTIONS: Play with a partner and decide who goes first. Each player chooses either paper clips or buttons as game markers. One player tosses the number cube, reads the number, and counts out that many of his or her game markers onto one of the spaces for that number on the game board. Players take turns until the game board is filled. The player who has filled more spaces on the game board wins.

86

Name _____

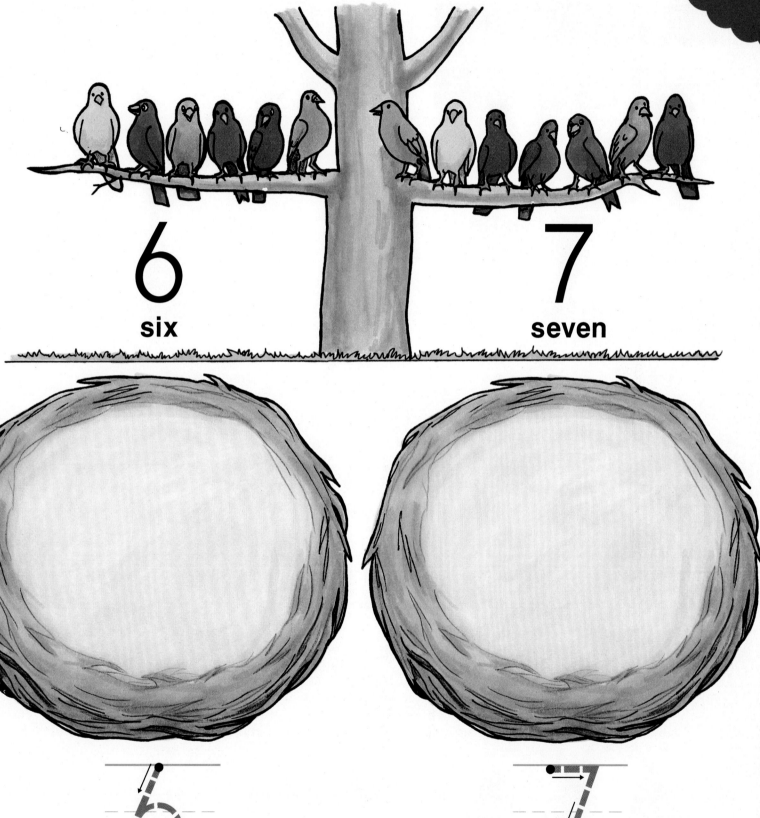

6

six

7

seven

Place counters in the nests to show how many. Draw
the counters in the nests. Trace the numbers.

© Harcourt

87

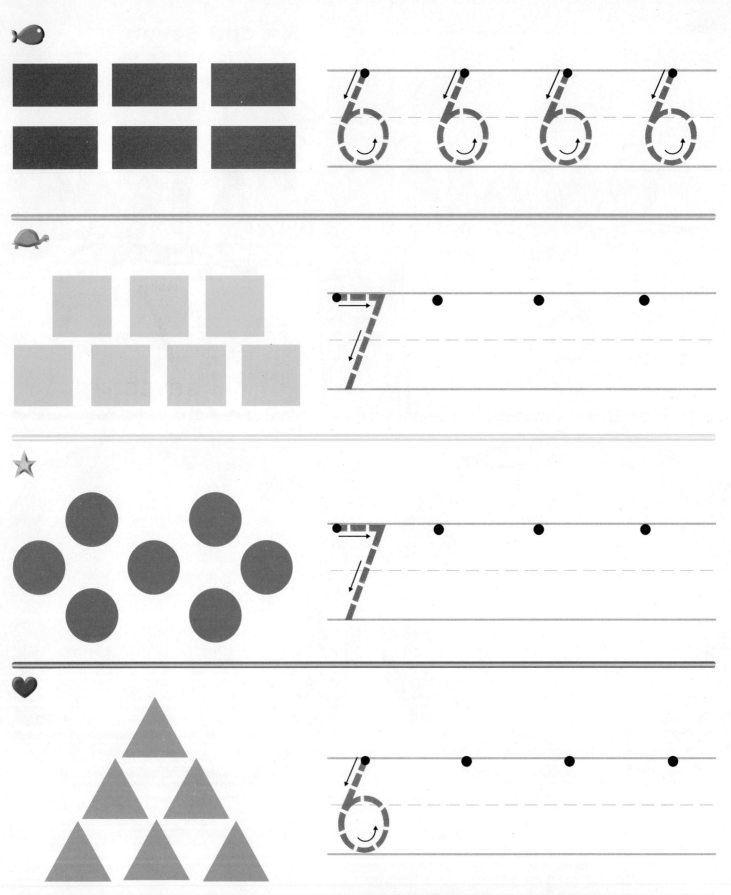

🐟 🐢 ⭐ ❤️ Count the shapes in the group.
Write the number.

🏠 **HOME ACTIVITY** • Remind your child that there are seven days in the week. Say the days together. Have your child raise one finger for each day and then count the raised fingers.

Name _____

Eight and Nine

🐟 **eight**   8

🐢 **nine**   9

⭐

❤️

🌼

🦋

🐟🐢 Count the dots in the group. Trace and write the number.
⭐❤️🌼🦋 How many are in the picture? Count. Write the number.

© Harcourt

89

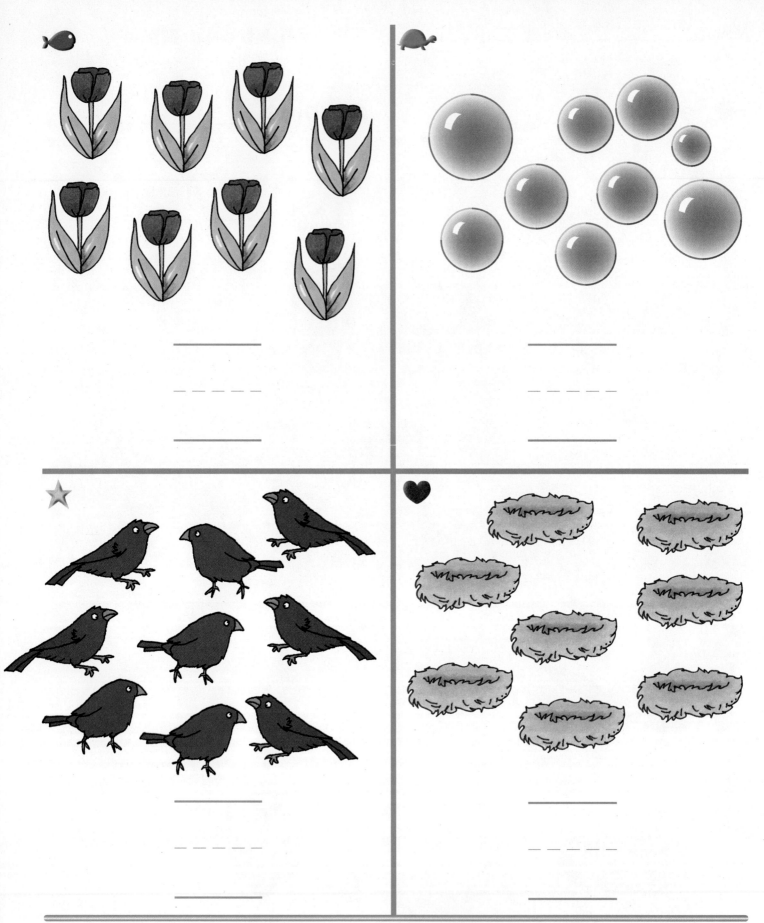

_____

- - - - - - - -

_____

🐟 🐢 ⭐ ❤ Count. Write the number that tells how many.

🏠 **HOME ACTIVITY** • Challenge your child to arrange 9 pennies in different ways, such as in a row, column, or square.

10
ten

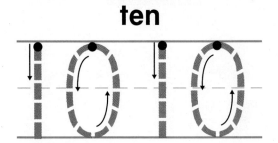

 Count the bees. Trace the number.

Draw more bees to make a group of 10.

10

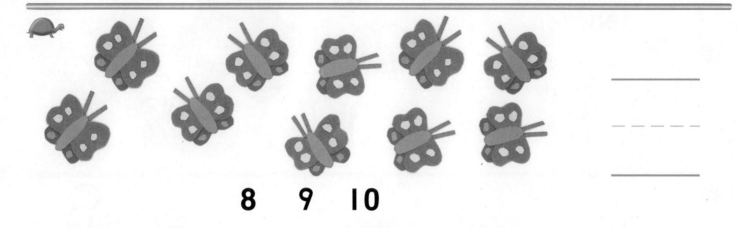

8　9　10

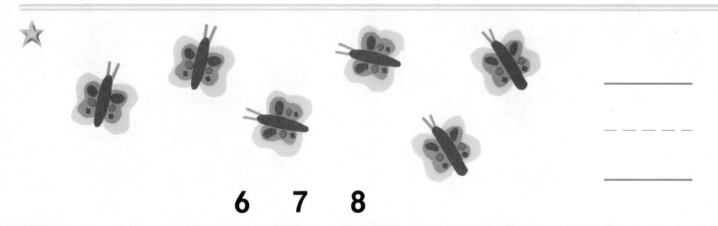

6　7　8

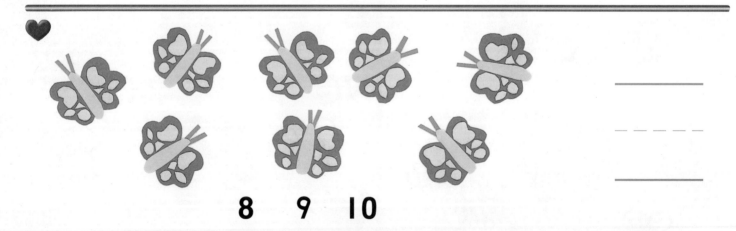

8　9　10

Write the number 10.
Count the butterflies. Circle the number that tells how many. Write the number.

HOME ACTIVITY • Have your child count his or her toes and write the number that tells how many.

© Harcourt

Connect 10 cubes. Then make one break to get two groups—one with more cubes than the other. Put the groups on the work space. For each group, draw the cubes and write the number. Circle the number that is greater. Use different numbers to make 10 each time.

Connect 10 cubes. Then make one break to get two groups—one with more cubes than the other. Put the groups on the work space. For each group, draw the cubes and write the number. Circle the number that is less. Use different numbers to make 10 each time.

HOME ACTIVITY • Have your child use pennies to show the number of people in your home at two different times of the day. Have him or her write the numbers. Ask if one number is more or if they are the same.

Name _____

✓ Review

6   7   8

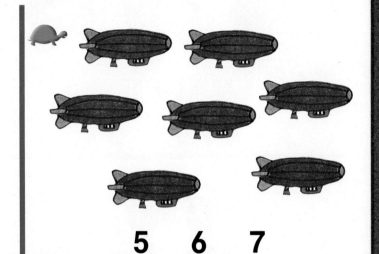

5   6   7

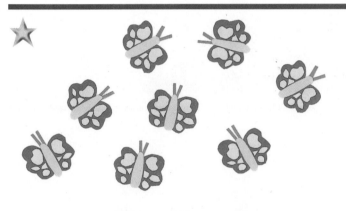

7   8   9

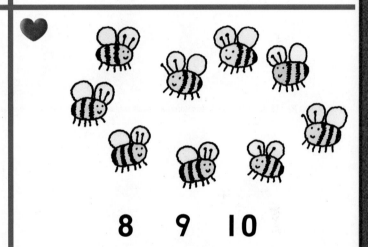

8   9   10

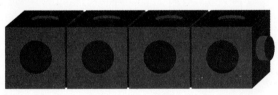

_____   _____

_ _ _ _ _ _   _ _ _ _ _ _

_____

🐟🐢⭐❤ Count the objects in the groups. Circle the number that tells
how many.
🌸 Count the cubes in each group and write the numbers. Circle the
number that is greater.

✔ Cumulative Review

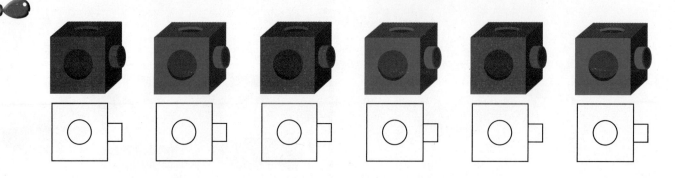

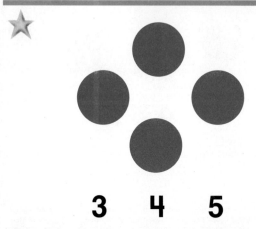

3 4 5

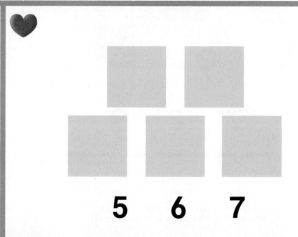

5 6 7

🐟 Read the pattern. Color the cubes to copy the pattern.
🐢 Draw lines to match the animals in the group. Compare the groups. Circle the group that has fewer.
⭐ ❤ Count the shapes. Circle the number that tells how many.
🌸 Count the bees. Draw more bees to make a group of ten.

Name _____

5 6 ___ 8 9 10

5 ___ 7 8 ___ 10

___ 6 7 ___ 9 10

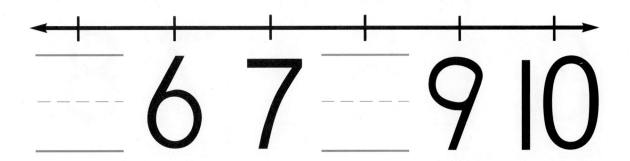

© Harcourt

97

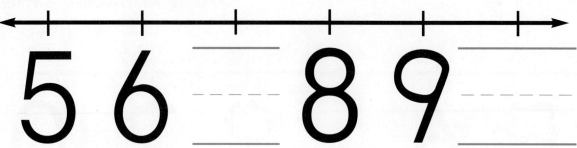

$5\ 6\ \_\_\ 8\ 9\ \_\_$

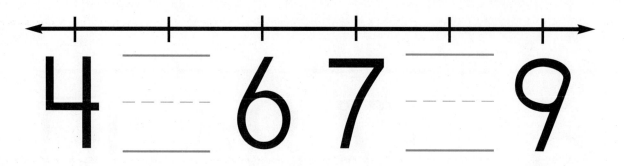

$4\ \_\_\ 6\ 7\ \_\_\ 9$

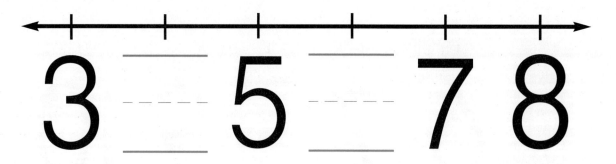

$3\ \_\_\ 5\ \_\_\ 7\ 8$

 Write the number that is before 8.
Write the number that is after 9.

Write the number that is after 4.
Write the number that is before 9.

⭐ Write the number that is after 3.
Write the number that is before 7.

🔶 **HOME ACTIVITY** • Ask your child to use the words *before* and *after* to describe numbers on a number line.

Write Numbers 0 to 10

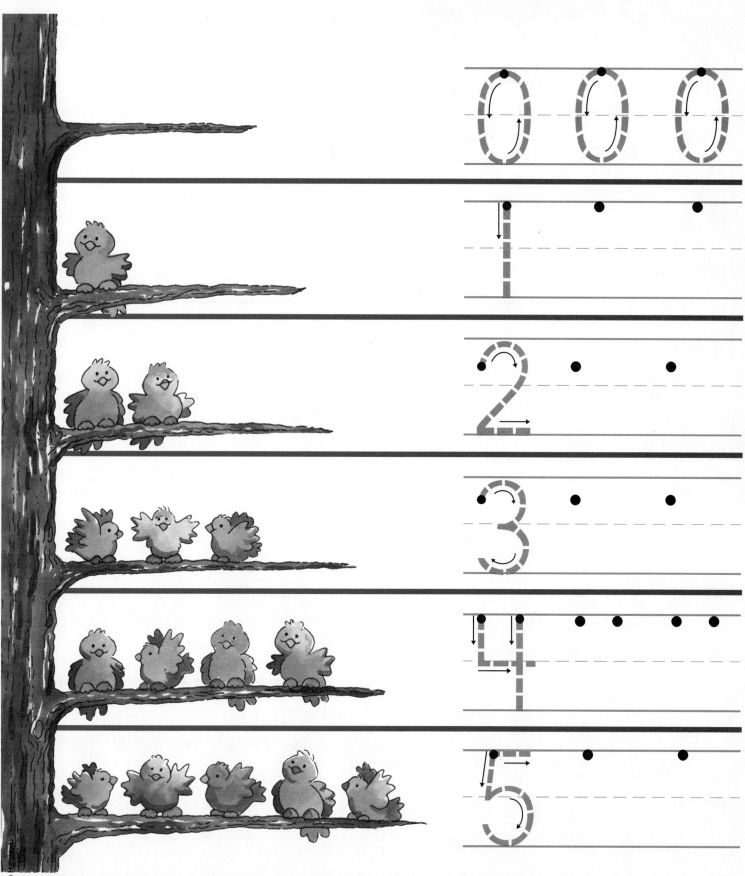

Trace the number that means none in a group. Now, count the birds and
write the number that tells how many birds in each group.

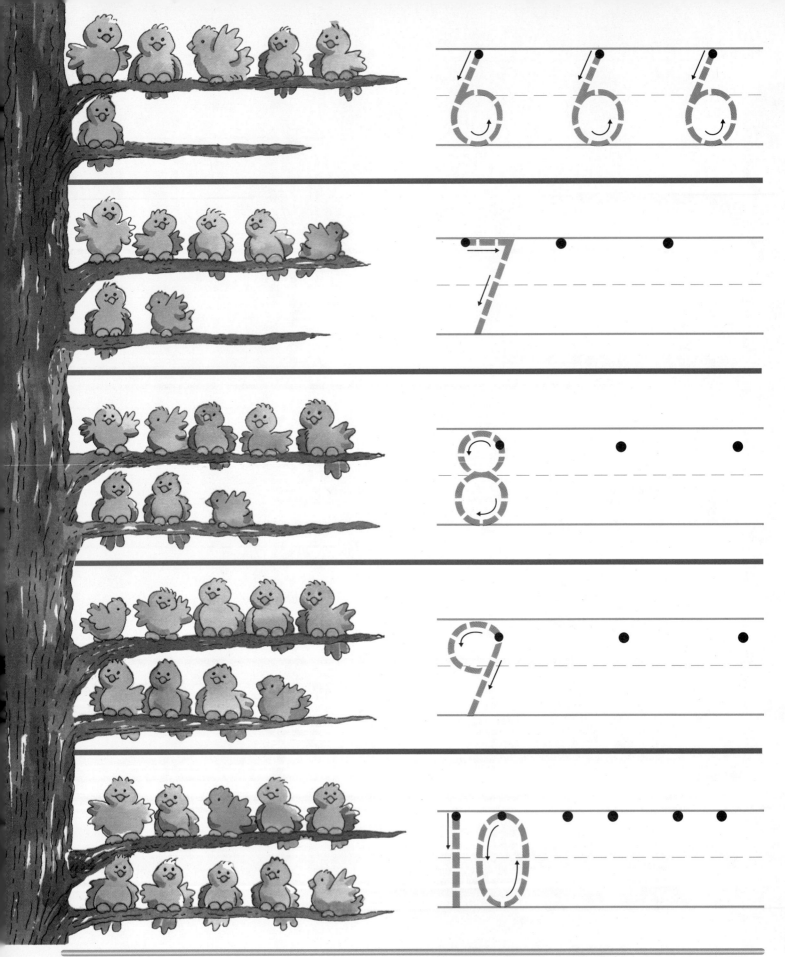

Count the birds and write the number that tells how many birds in each group.

 HOME ACTIVITY • Have your child count aloud from 0 to 10. Then have him or her try counting from 10 to 0.

100

Algebra:
Missing Numbers

4 5 6 ■ 8

2
7

🐢

☐ 7 8 9 10

5
6

⭐

0 1 ■ 3 4

2
5

♥

3 4 5 ☐ 7

3
6

🐟 🐢 ⭐ ♥ **Circle the missing number.**

© Harcourt

7   6   5   ⬛   3 | 4 |
                           | 8 |

9   8   7   ⬛   5 | 10 |
                           | 6 |

⭐

⬛   6   5   4   3 | 7 |
                           | 8 |

♥

10   ⬛   8   7   6 | 5 |
                           | 9 |

🐟 🐢 ⭐ ♥ Circle the missing number.

 HOME ACTIVITY • Say several numbers in order, leaving out one number. Ask your child to tell you what number is missing.

Name _____

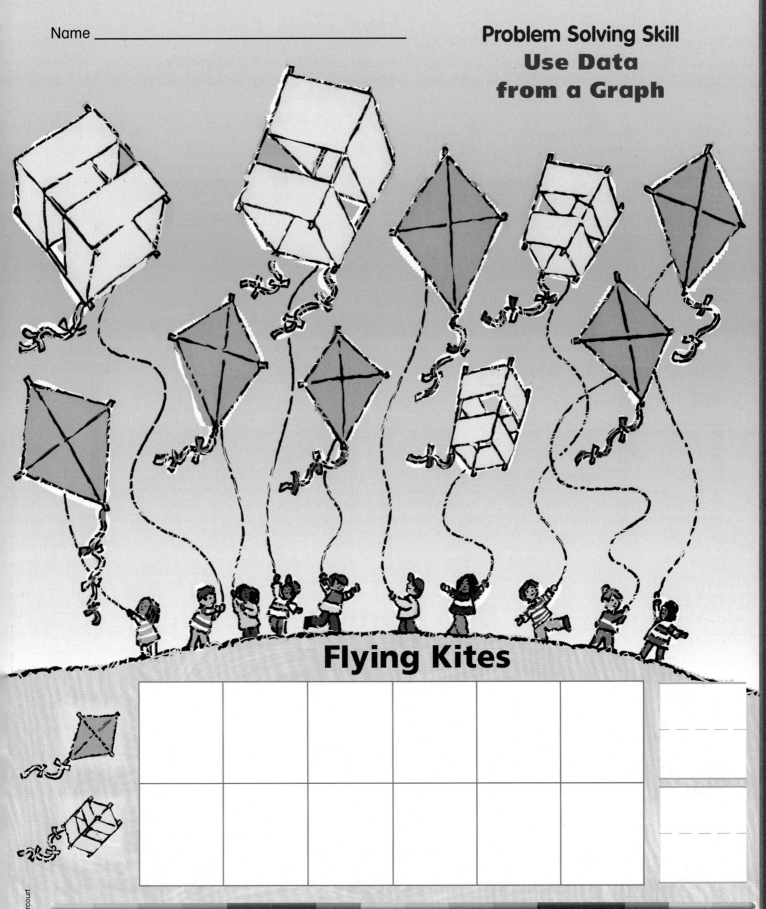

Flying Kites

Put an orange cube on each orange kite and a yellow cube on
each yellow kite. Move the cubes to the graph. Count the cubes
in each row and write the number. Are there more orange kites
or more yellow kites? Circle the number that is greater.

© Harcourt

103

Bird Homes

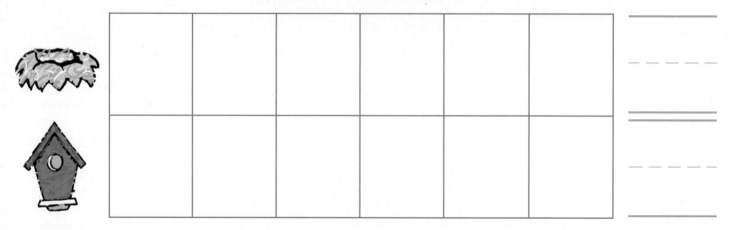

Put a red cube on each birdhouse and a yellow cube on each nest. Move the cubes to the graph. Count the cubes in each row and write the number. Are there more nests or more birdhouses? Circle the number that is less.

🏠 HOME ACTIVITY • Have your child find out whether each family member would rather have milk or juice and then use the information to draw a simple graph.

104

CIRCLE A GROUP
DRAW A GROUP

By _____

HOME ACTIVITY • This book will help review the numbers 6 to 10. Invite your child to share this book with you.

Draw a group of 6 bees.

3

Circle the group of 6 trees.

2

Circle the group of 7 ants.

4

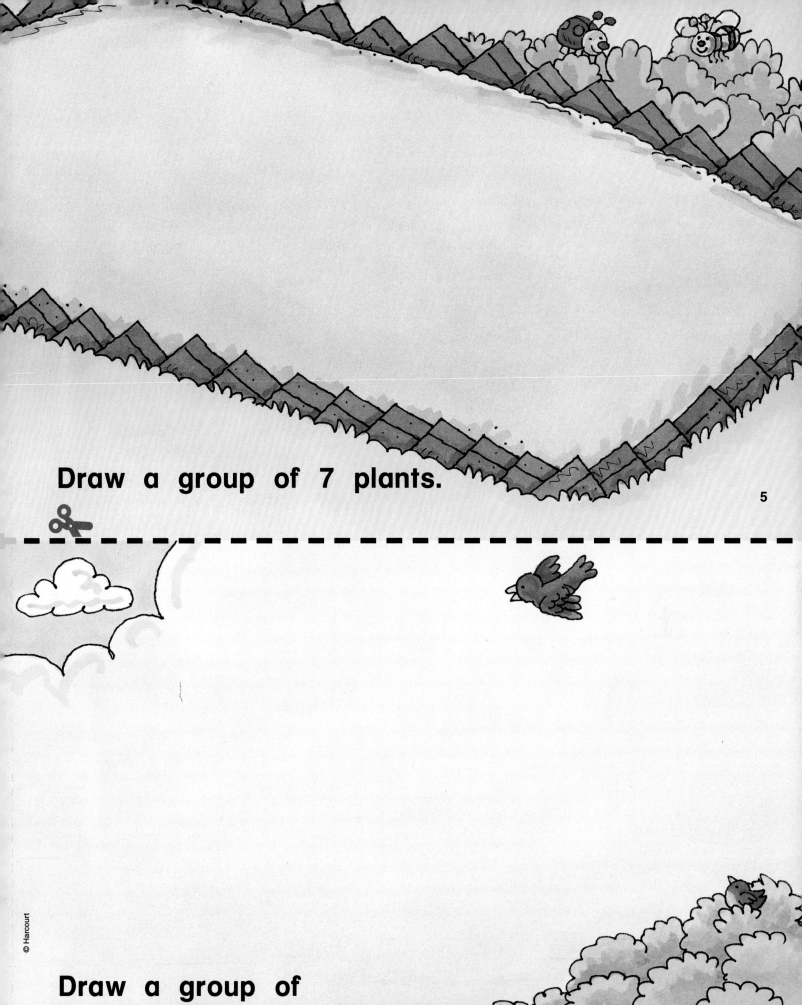

Draw a group of 7 plants.

5

Draw a group of 8 balloons.

7

Circle the group of 8 raccoons.

6

✂

Circle the group of 9 frogs.

8

© Harcourt

Draw a group of 9 logs.

Draw a group of 10 tops.

11

Circle the group of 10 raindrops.

10

6   7   8   9   10

Name _____

✔️ Review

🐟

___ 6 7 ___ 9 10

🐢

10 ⬛ 8 7 6

$\boxed{\begin{array}{c} 5 \\ 9 \end{array}}$

⭐

Flying Kites

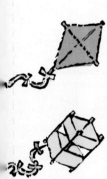
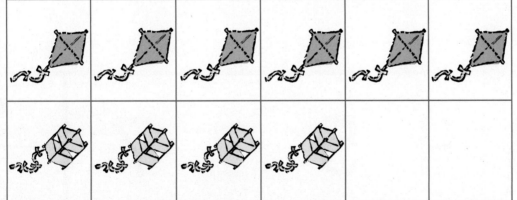

_____
- - - - -
_____

_____
- - - - -
_____

© Harcourt

🐟 Write the number that is before 6. Write the number that is after 7.
🐢 Circle the missing number.
⭐ Count the kites in each row of the graph and write the numbers. Are there
more orange kites or yellow kites? Circle the number that is greater.

Cumulative Review

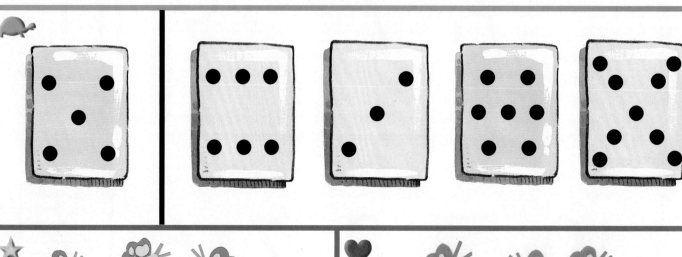

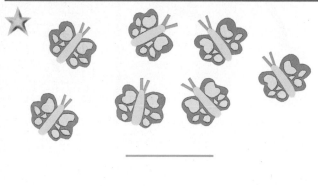

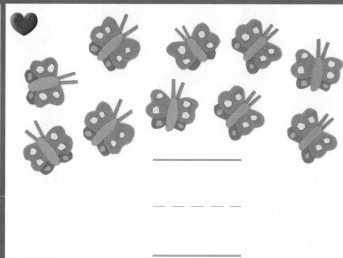

 3 4 5 [ ] 7

🐟 Color the cubes to show what most likely comes next.

🐢 Look at the card with 5 dots at the beginning of the row. Without counting, circle the card with fewer dots.

⭐ 💜 Count the butterflies. Write the number.

🌸 Circle the missing number.

106

Name _____

✔ Test

_____
_ _ _ _ _ _ _ _
_____

_____   _____
_ _ _ _ _ _   _ _ _ _ _ _
_____   _____

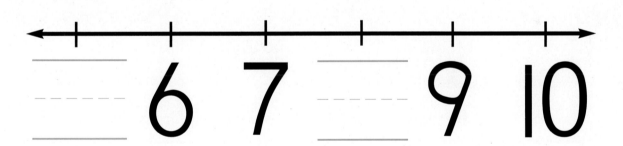

_____ 6 7 _____ 9 10

6 7   9 10 | 5 / 8

🐟 Count the shapes. Write how many.
🐢 Count the cubes in each group and write the numbers.
Circle the number that is greater.
⭐ Write the number that is before 6. Write the number that is after 7.
❤ Circle the missing number.

107

CHALLENGE
In the Park

Flowers, Birds, and Butterflies

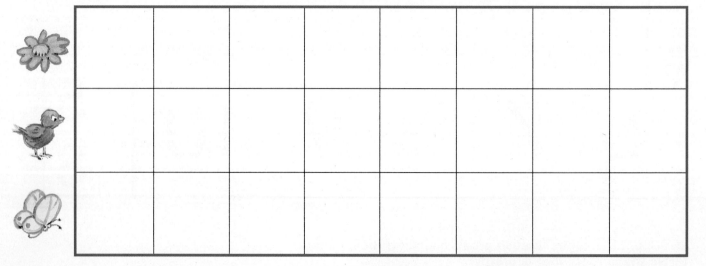

Color the boxes in the graph to show how many are in the park.

 CHAPTER 5

Geometry and Fractions

Harcourt

🐟 🐢 ⭐ ❤️ **Circle the shapes that are the same.**

Photography Credits:

All photography by Harcourt photographers listed, © Harcourt: Weronica Ankarorn, Victoria Bowen, Ken Kinzie, Sheri O'Neal, Quebecor Imaging, and Terry Sinclair.

Nan Brooks: 112; **Heidi King:** 117, 129, 130; **Jill Meyerhoff:** 123; **Stephanie Peterson:** 117, 118, 124, 125, 126; **Pattie Silver:** 120; **Valerie Sokolova:** cover; **Paige Billin-Frye:** storybook.

© Harcourt

SCHOOL HOME CONNECTION

Dear Family,

Today we started a new chapter, Geometry and Fractions. We will learn to recognize and name geometric shapes and equal parts.

Love,

_____

Solid Figures	**Plane Shapes**
cone	circle
sphere	triangle
cylinder	square
cube	rectangle

- Choose one of the solid figures listed, and help your child find objects that have that shape.

BOOKS TO SHARE

To read about shapes with your child, look for these books at your local library.

Sea Shapes, by Suse MacDonald. Harcourt, 1994.

What Is Round? by Rebecca Kai-Dotlich. HarperCollins, 1999.

Color Zoo, by Lois Ehlert. HarperCollins, 1989.

Visit *The Learning Site* for additional ideas and activities.
www.harcourtschool.com

Math Game

MATERIALS: 2 game markers, paper clip, pencil

DIRECTIONS: Play with a partner. Place your game markers at START and decide who goes first. Players take turns spinning the spinner. Each player names the shape the spinner lands on and moves his or her game marker to the closest object with the same shape. The first player to reach END wins.

112

sphere   **cone**   **cube**   **cylinder**

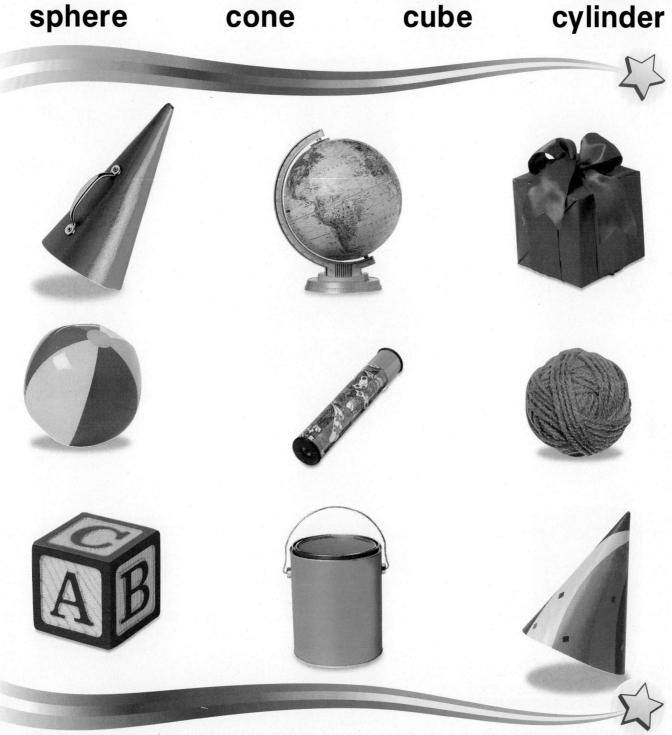

Use blue to circle the objects shaped like spheres.
Use red to circle the objects shaped like cones.
Use yellow to circle the objects shaped like cubes.
Use green to circle the objects shaped like cylinders.

Use blue to circle the objects shaped like spheres.
Use red to circle the objects shaped like cones.
Use yellow to circle the objects shaped like cubes.
Use green to circle the objects shaped like cylinders.

⬟ **HOME ACTIVITY** • Have your child use the words *sphere*, *cube*, *cylinder*, and *cone* to tell you about the objects on this page.

114

Name _____

Move Solid Figures

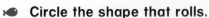

- Circle the shape that rolls.
- Circle the shape that stacks.
- Circle the shape that slides.
- Circle the shape that rolls and slides.

© Harcourt

115

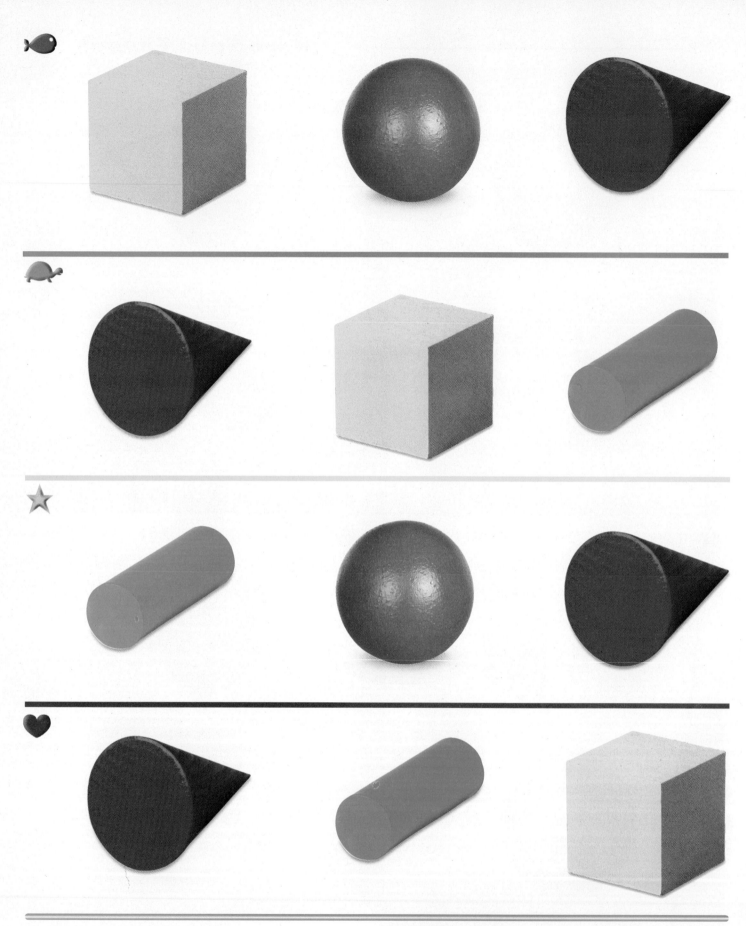

🐟 Circle the shapes that roll.
🐢 Circle the shapes that stack.
⭐ Circle the shapes that slide.
❤ Circle the shapes that stack and slide.

🏠 **HOME ACTIVITY** • Have your child find and name shapes in your home that roll, stack, or slide.

116

PROBLEM SOLVING

Look at the object at the beginning of the row. Color in the outline that matches the shape of the object.

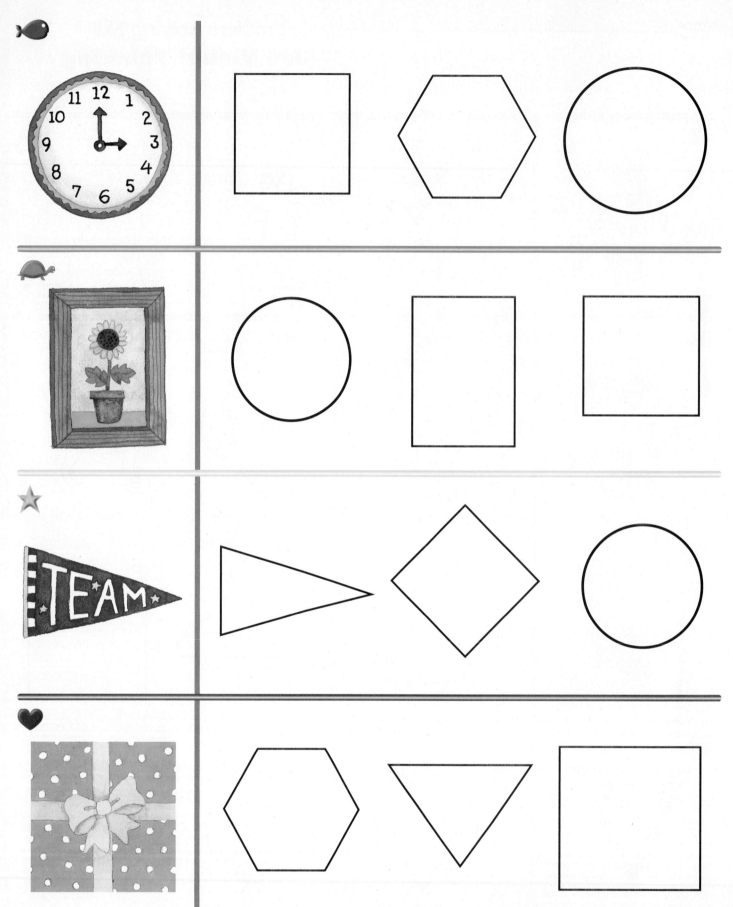

Look at the object at the beginning of the row. Color in the outline that matches the shape of the object.

HOME ACTIVITY • Have your child trace around objects to explore shapes and their outlines.

© Harcourt

118

Name _____ Algebra: **Sort Plane Shapes**

circle   **square**   **triangle**   **rectangle**

Use the words *curves*, *sides*, and *corners* to describe each shape.
Use orange to circle the shapes with curves.
Use purple to circle the shapes with four sides.
Use green to circle the shapes with three corners.

119

Color the circles yellow. Color the squares and rectangles blue. Color the triangles green.

HOME ACTIVITY • Go on a "Shape Hunt." Help your child find and name shapes in your home.

120

Name _____

Color the triangles blue, color the squares red,
and color the rectangles orange.

121

Use plane shapes to finish the puzzle. What shapes did you use? Use the same color to color the shapes that are alike.

⬠ **HOME ACTIVITY** • Have your child find triangles, squares, and rectangles in your home and community.

© Harcourt

122

Name _____

✅ **Review**

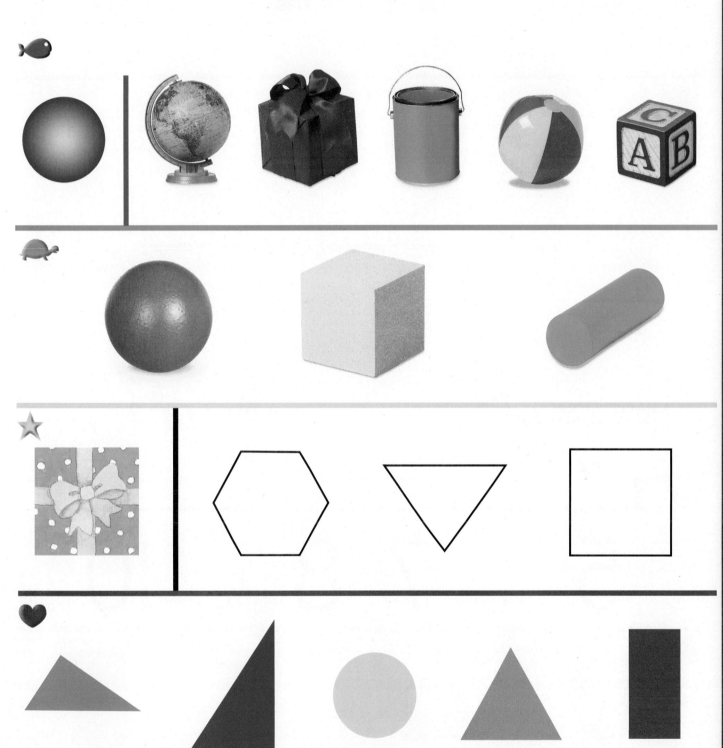

🐟 Look at the shape at the beginning of the row. Circle the objects shaped like spheres.
🐢 Circle the shapes that stack.
⭐ Look at the object at the beginning of the row. Color the outline that matches the shape of the object.
♥ Circle the shapes with three corners.

123

✓ Cumulative Review

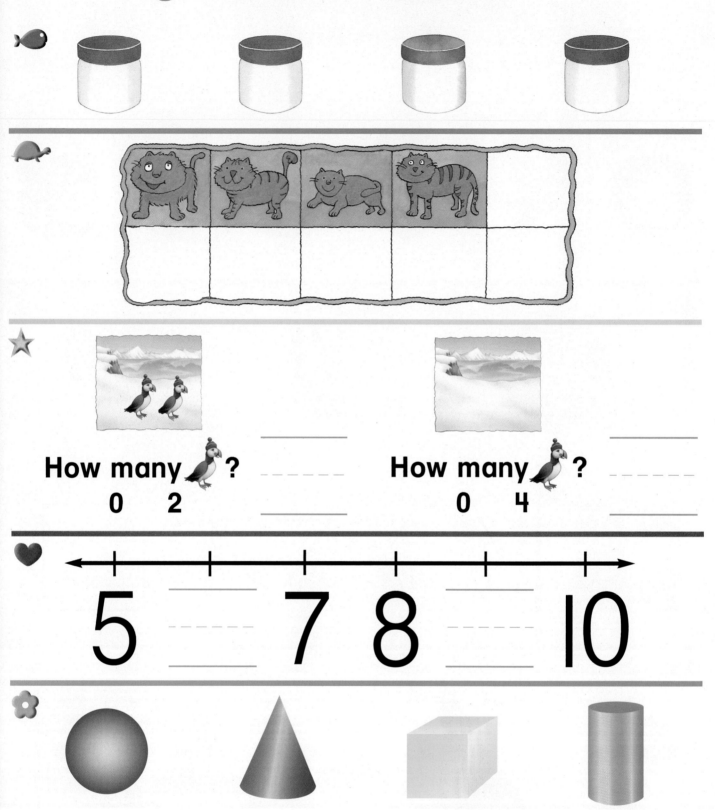

How many 🐧**?**
0   2

How many 🐧**?**
0   4

5   7 8   10

🐟 Mark an X on the object that does not belong.
🐢 Color one box for each cat.
⭐ Count the puffins. Circle the number that tells how many.
Then write the number.
❤ Write the number that is after 5. Write the number that is before 10.
🌸 Use red to circle the cone. Use green to circle the cylinder.

Name _____

Symmetry

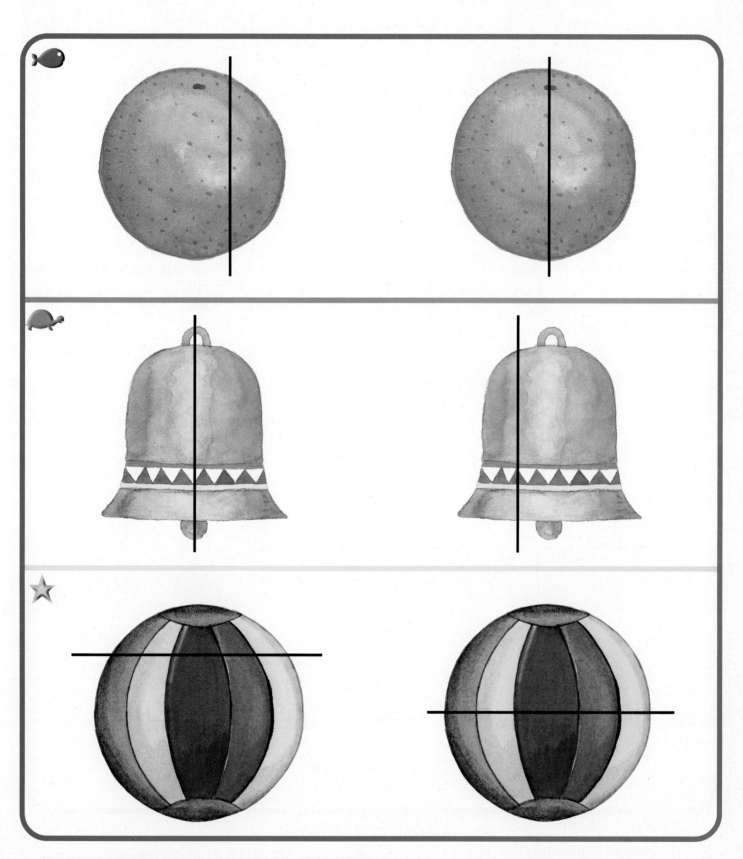

Circle the objects that have a line that
divides them into two matching parts.

Circle the objects that have a line that divides them into two matching parts.

 HOME ACTIVITY • Cut out a paper square or circle. Help your child fold the shape to show two matching parts.

126

  Circle the shape that shows equal parts.
How do you know?

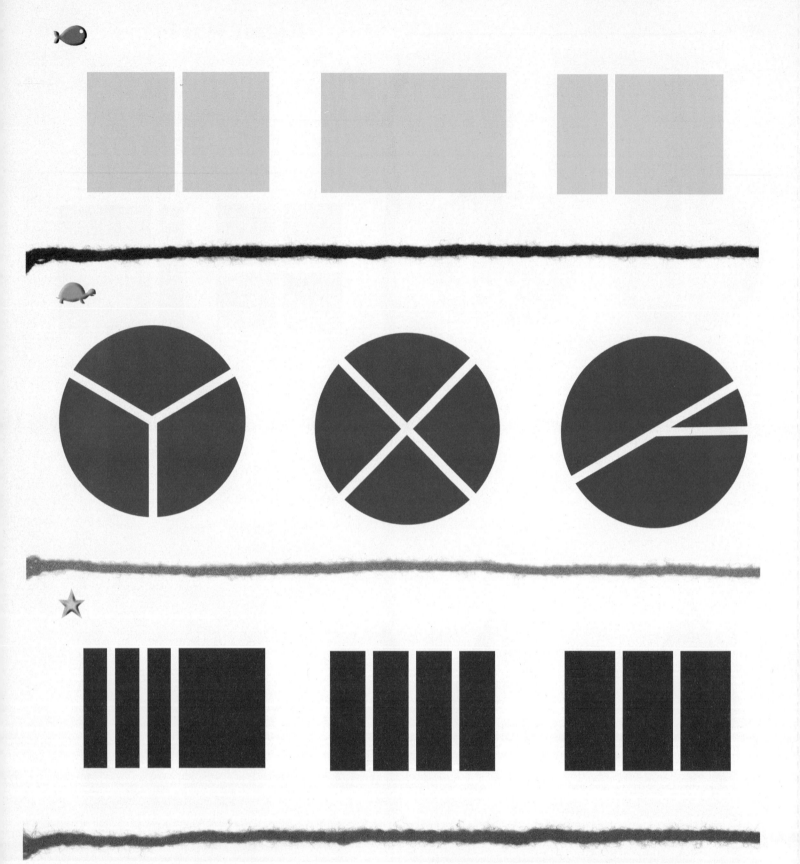

🐟 Circle the shape that is divided into two equal parts. How do you know?

🐢 Circle the shape that is divided into three equal parts. How do you know?

⭐ Circle the shape that is divided into four equal parts. How do you know?

⬟ **HOME ACTIVITY** • Cut some food items into equal parts and others into unequal parts. Have your child point out the items that are cut into equal parts.

128

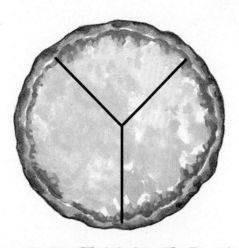
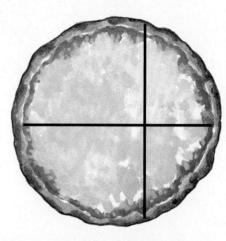

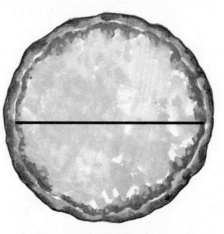

Use your pizza pieces to find the pizza that
shows 2 equal parts, or halves. Color one half.
Use your pizza pieces to find the pizza that
shows 4 equal parts, or fourths. Color one fourth.

Use green to color one part of each shape. Use red to circle the shapes that show one half. Use blue to circle the shapes that show one fourth.

HOME ACTIVITY • As you prepare meals or snacks, show your child how you divide foods, such as fruits and sandwiches, into halves or fourths.

Find the Shapes

By _____

HOME ACTIVITY • This book will help review shapes. Invite your child to share this book with you. Have him or her point to each shape.

1

Find the objects shaped
like triangles.

3

Find the objects shaped like squares.

2

Find the objects shaped like circles.

4

Find the objects shaped like rectangles.

Find the objects shaped like cubes.

Find the objects shaped like circles, squares, triangles, and rectangles.

6

Find the objects shaped like spheres.

8

Find the objects shaped like cones.

9

Find the objects shaped like cubes, spheres, cones, and cylinders.

11

Find the objects shaped like cylinders.

10

Tell about each shape.

12

Name _____

✓ Review

 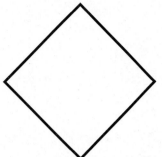 

  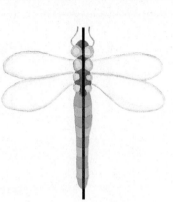 

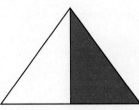 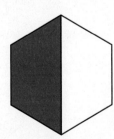 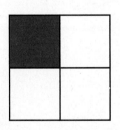 

 Color the circle red. Color the square yellow. Color the triangle blue.
Color the rectangle green.

Circle the pictures that have a line that makes two matching parts.

Circle the shapes that show equal parts.

Circle the shapes that show one half red. Draw a line under the shape
that shows one fourth red.

131

Cumulative Review

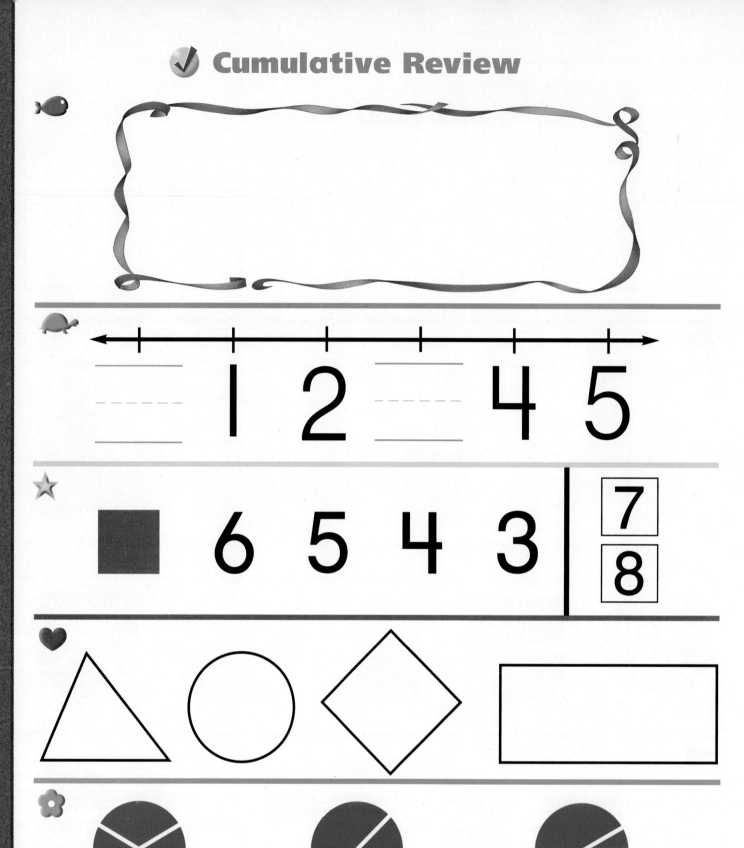

1 2 __ 4 5

6 5 4 3 | 7 / 8

Use counters to make your own pattern. Draw your pattern.
Write the number that is before 1. Write the number that is after 2.
Circle the missing number.
Color the circle red. Color the csquare yellow. Color the triangle blue. Color the rectangle green.
Circle the shape that is divided into three equal parts.

© Harcourt

Name _____

✅ Test

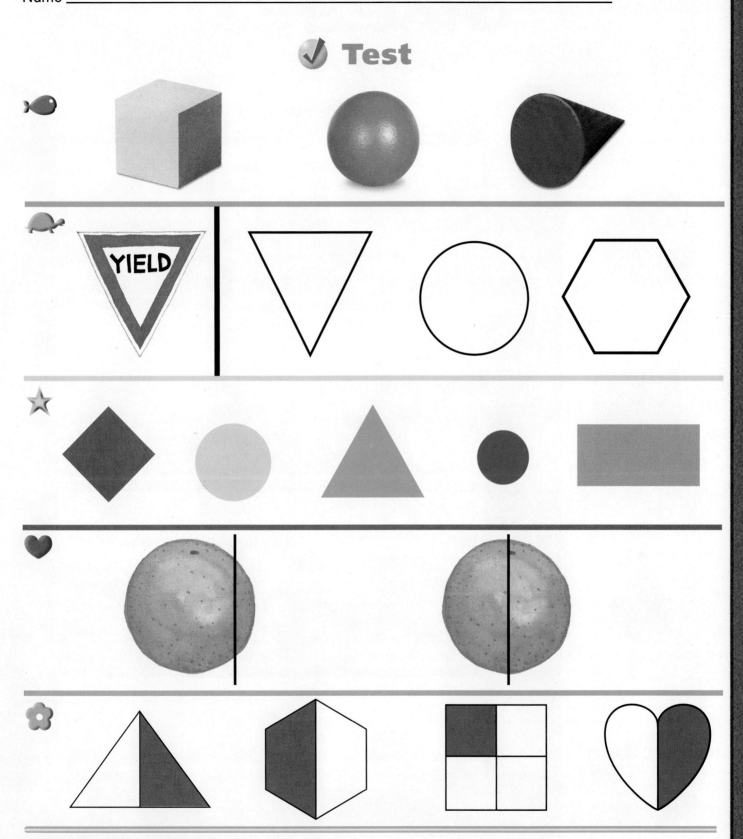

Circle the shapes that roll.

Look at the object at the beginning of the row. Color in the outline that matches the shape of the object.

Circle the square.

Circle the orange that has a line that makes two matching parts.

Circle the shapes that show one half red. Draw a line under the shape that shows one fourth red.

133

CHALLENGE
Shape Prints

Circle the solid figures that could make the plane shape print.

Numbers 10 to 30

HARCOURT Math

Harcourt

Circle the groups with ten animals.

Photography Credits:

All photography by Harcourt photographers listed, © Harcourt: Weronica Ankarorn, Victoria Bowen, Ken Kinzie, Sheri O'Neal, Quebecor Imaging, and Terry Sinclair.

Illustration Credits:

Paige Billin-Frye: Storybook; **Joe Boddy:** 138; **Daniel Del Valle:** 145, 146; **Patty Silver:** 139, 140, 141, 142; **Geraldo Suzan:** 143, 144; **Stan Tusan:** cvr, 136, 147, 148; **Jane Yamada:** 151, 152 .

SCHOOL HOME
CONNECTION

Dear Family,

Today we started a new chapter, *Numbers 10 to 30*. In this chapter, we will learn about numbers to 30 and how to see these numbers on ten frames.

Love,

_____

Vocabulary Power

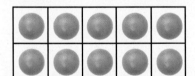

groups of 10 on ten-frames

The names for 11, 12, 13, and 15 may be harder for children to remember since they do not contain the familiar number names *one*, *two*, *three*, and *five*.

Visit *The Learning Site* for additional ideas and activities.
www.harcourtschool.com

ACTIVITY

• Count aloud often with your child.

BOOKS TO SHARE

To read about numbers with your child, look for these books at your local library.

Let's Count It Out, Jesse Bear,
by Nancy White Carlstrom. Simon & Schuster, 1996.

Count!
by Denise Fleming. Henry Holt, 1997.

Bears at the Beach,
by Niki Yektai. Millbrook, 1996.

© Harcourt

137

MATERIALS: a different colored pencil for each player
DIRECTIONS: Play with a partner. Each player takes a turn drawing lines to connect the numbers 10 to 30 in order. If one player cannot continue, the partner takes over and draws lines as far as possible. The first player to reach 30 wins.

Name _____

ten

PROBLEM SOLVING

🐟 Place 10 cubes on the ten frame. Trace the number.

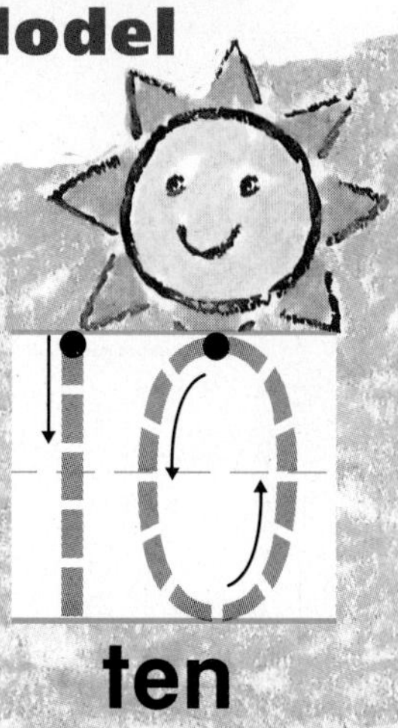

🐢 Use cubes to model the number that is 1 less than 9.
Write the number.

⭐ Use cubes to model the number that is 2 more than 8.
Write the number.

© Harcourt

139

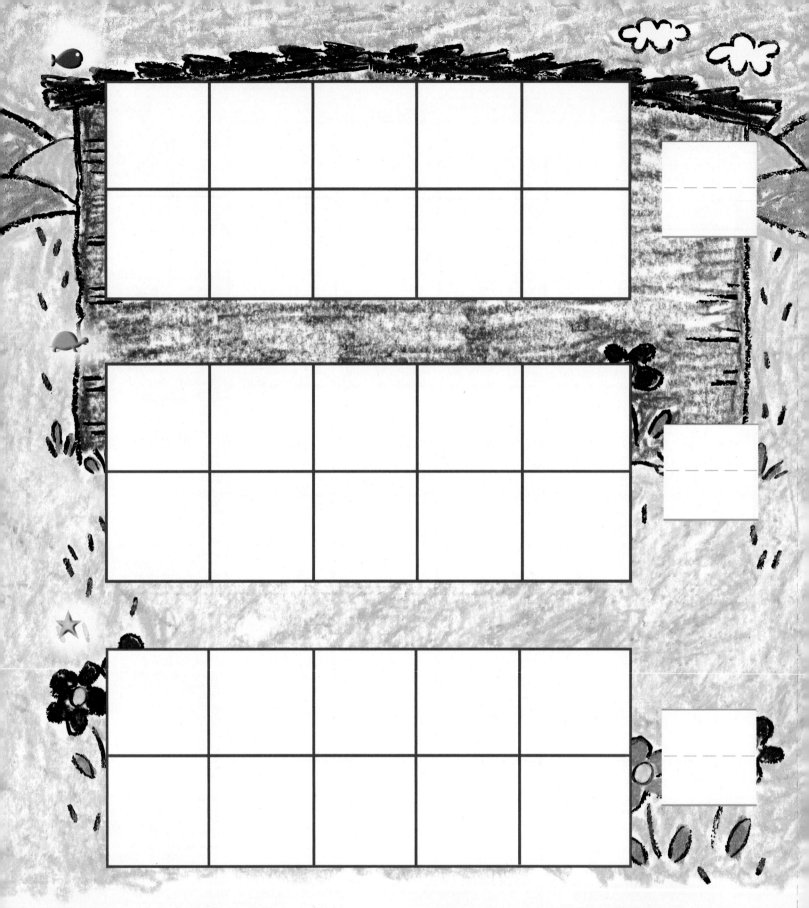

Use cubes to model the number that is
1 less than 10. Write the number.

Use cubes to model the number that is
1 more than 9. Write the number.

Use cubes to model the number that is
3 more than 7. Write the number.

HOME ACTIVITY • Draw a ten frame on a
sheet of paper. Model numbers from 1 to 10,
using small objects such as dried beans. Each
time, ask your child if the ten frame shows a
group of 10.

140

© Harcourt

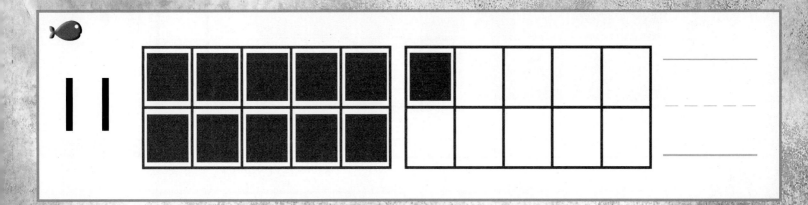

🐟 11

🐢 12

⭐ 13

Say the number. Count the color tiles. Write the number.

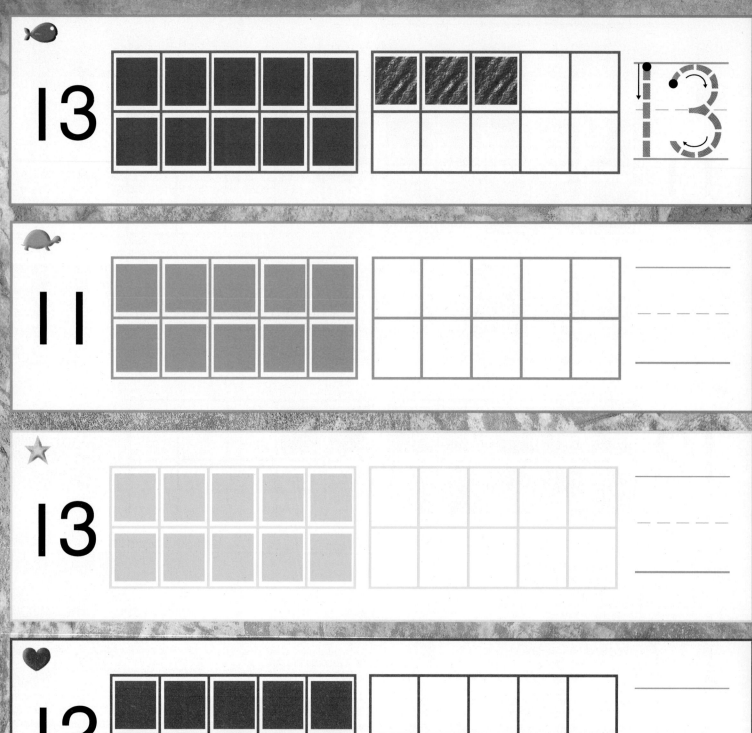

🐟 Draw more color tiles to make 13.
Write the number.

🐢 Draw more color tiles to make 11.
Write the number.

⭐ Draw more color tiles to make 13.
Write the number.

❤ Draw more color tiles to make 12.
Write the number.

🏠 **HOME ACTIVITY** • Draw two ten frames side by side on a sheet of paper. Have your child show the numbers 11 and 12, using small objects such as buttons.

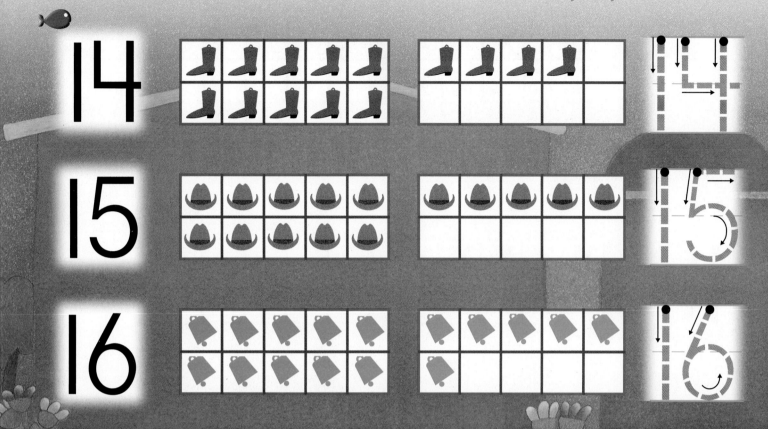

14

15

16

14

15

16

🐟 Count the objects. Trace the numbers.
🐢 Draw more Xs to show the numbers. Write the numbers.

© Harcourt

143

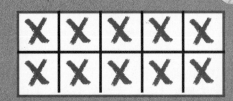 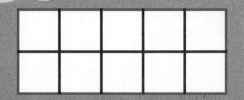

15

13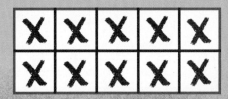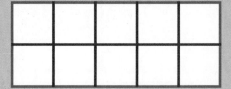

16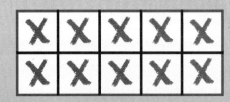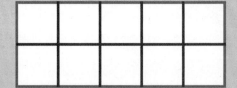

14

Draw more Xs to show the number. Write the number.

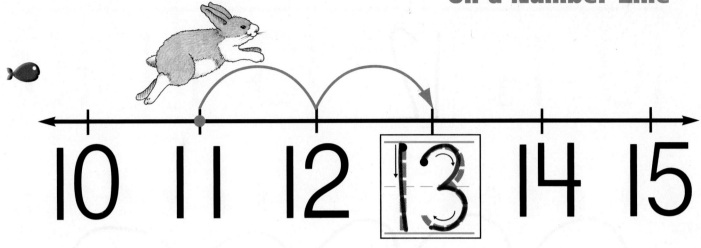

10 11 12 13 14 15

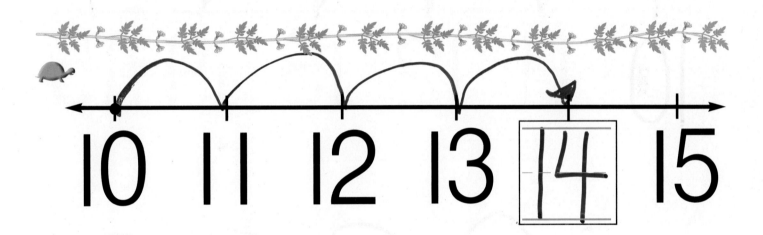

10 11 12 13 14 15

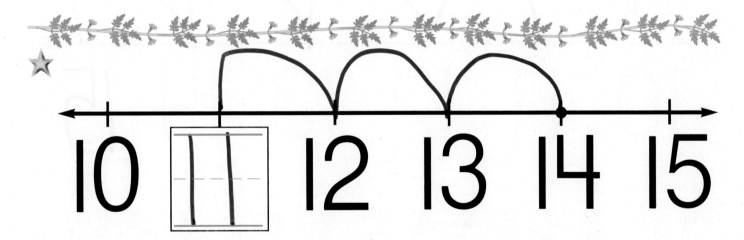

10 11 12 13 14 15

Start at 11. Count 2 numbers forward. Write the number.
Start at 10. Count 4 numbers forward. Write the number.
Start at 14. Count 3 numbers back. Write the number.

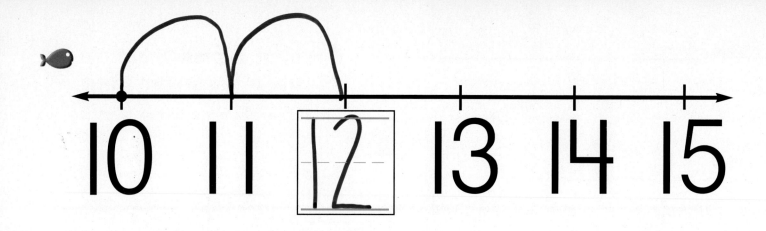

10 11 12 13 14 15

10 11 12 13 14 15

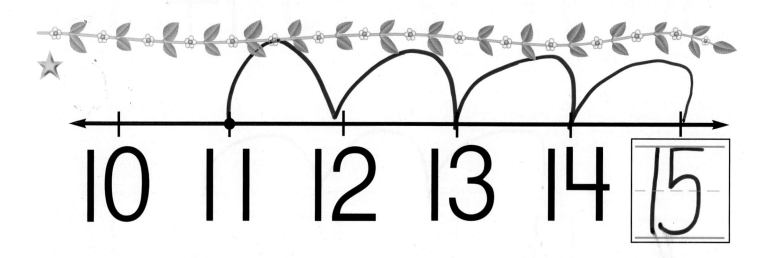

10 11 12 13 14 15

🐟 Start at 10. Count 2 numbers forward.
Write the number.

🐢 Start at 15. Count 5 numbers back.
Write the number.

⭐ Start at 11. Count 4 numbers forward.
Write the number.

HOME ACTIVITY • Draw a number line from 0 to 16. Invite your child to read the numbers on the number line.

Name _____

17 and 18

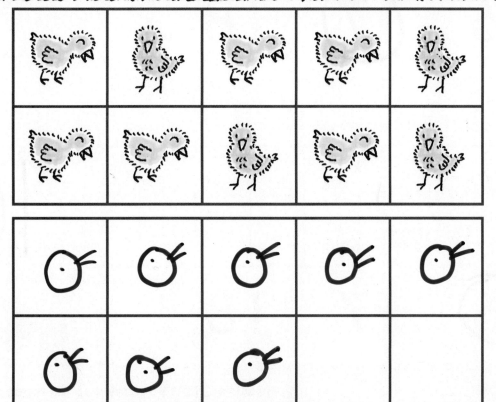

🐟 Draw more chicks to show 7 more than 10. Trace the number.
🐢 Draw more chicks to show 8 more than 10. Trace the number.

147

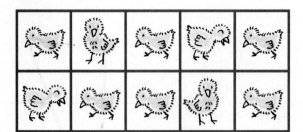 

16　　17　　(18)

16　　(17)　　18

  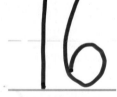

(16)　　17　　18

Count the chicks.
Circle the number that tells how many.
Write the number.

HOME ACTIVITY • Draw two ten frames on a sheet of paper. Have your child use coins or other small objects to show 17 and 18.

Name _____

✔️ **Review**

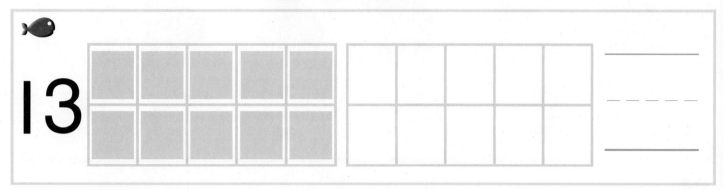

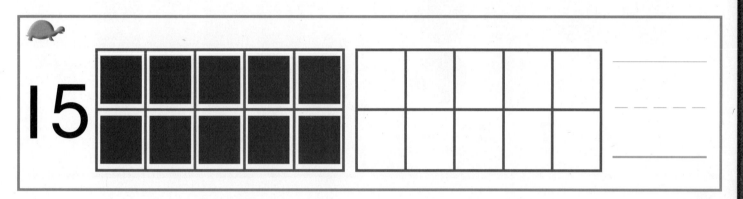

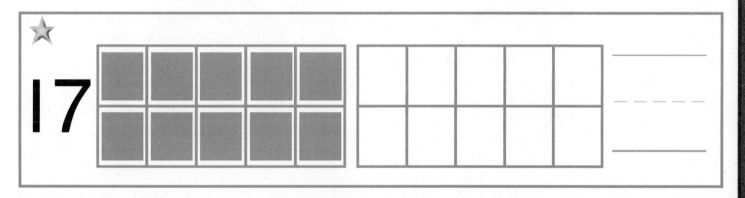

10   11   ⬚   13   14   15

© Harcourt

🐟 Draw more color tiles to make 13. Write the number.
🐢 Draw more color tiles to make 15. Write the number.
⭐ Draw more color tiles to make 17. Write the number.
❤️ Start at 10. Count two numbers forward. Write the number.

✔️ Cumulative Review

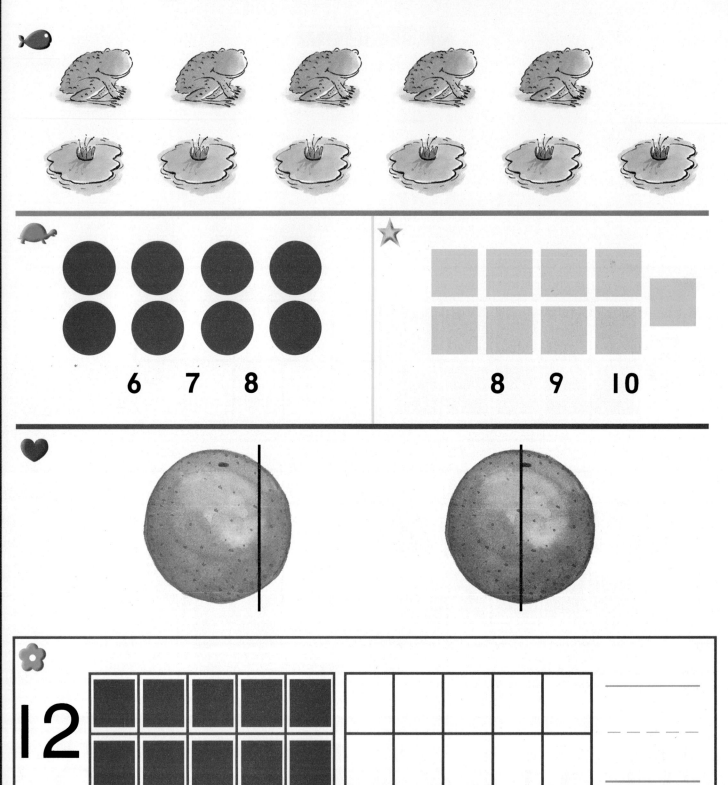

6   7   8

8   9   10

12

Draw lines to match the objects in the two groups. Compare the groups.
Circle the group that has more.
Count. Circle the number that tells how many.
Circle the orange that is divided into two matching parts.
Draw more color tiles to make 12. Write the number.

Name _____

Shirts

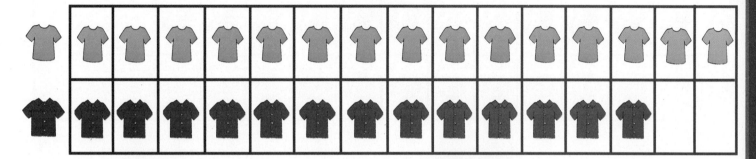

 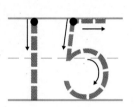  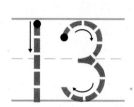

Weather

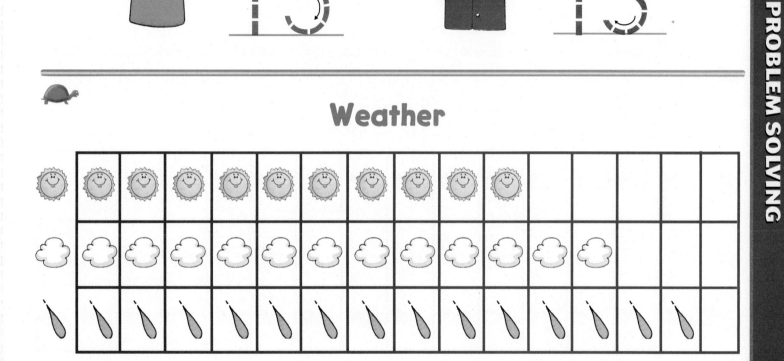

 Count and write how many. Circle the number that shows
more. Mark an X on the number that shows fewer.
 Count and write how many. Circle the number that shows
the most. Mark an X on the number that shows the fewest.

Pets

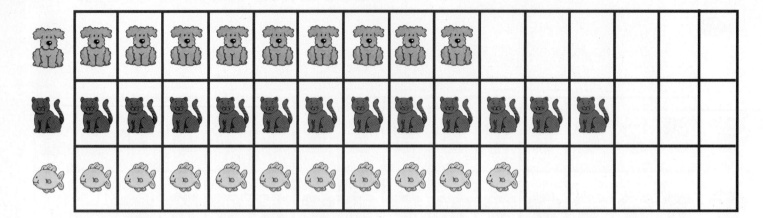

 _____

_____

 _____

_____

 _____

_____

Shoes

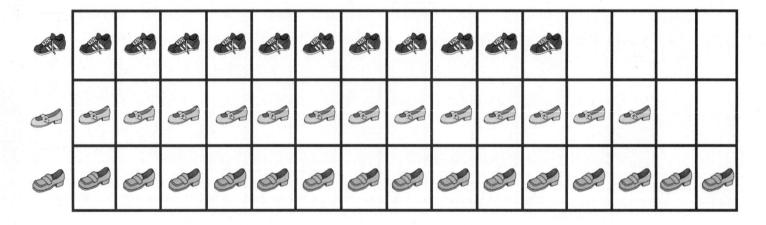

 _____

_____

 _____

_____

 _____

_____

Count and write how many. Circle the number that shows the most. Mark an X on the number that shows the fewest.

HOME ACTIVITY • Ask your child to tell you about the graphs on this page.

152

🐟 🐢 Count. Trace the number.

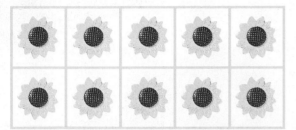 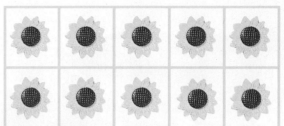 

18   19   (20)

18   19   20

18   19   20

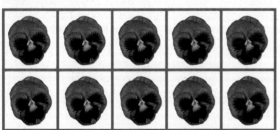 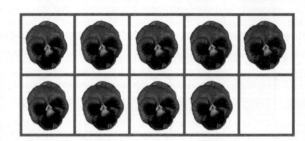

18   19   20

Count the objects. Circle the number that tells how many. Write the number.

HOME ACTIVITY • Set out small objects in groups of 11 to 20, and invite your child to count them.

© Harcourt

154

Name _____

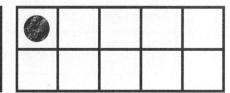

21

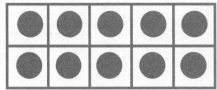
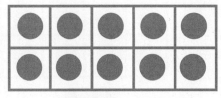
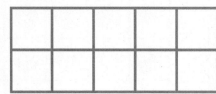

22

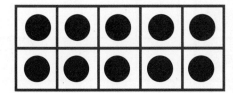
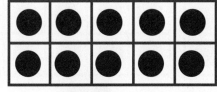
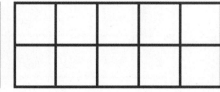

23

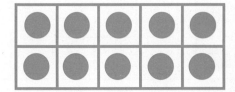
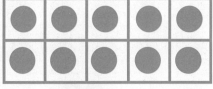

24

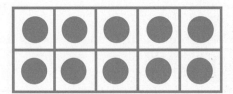
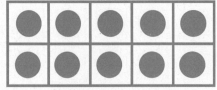

25

Draw more counters to make 21.
Draw more counters to make 22.
Draw more counters to make 23.
Draw more counters to make 24.
Draw more counters to make 25.

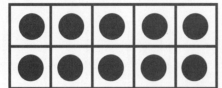 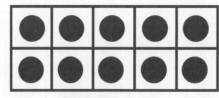 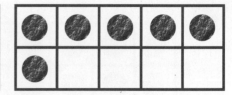

26

  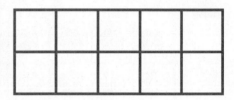

27

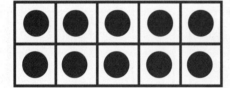  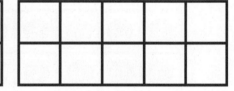

28

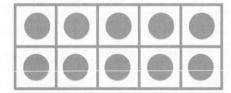  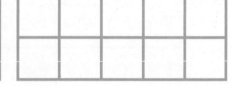

29

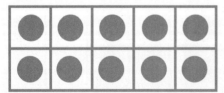 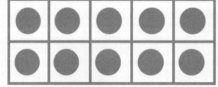 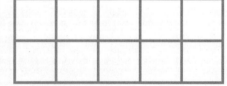

30

🐟 Draw more counters to make 26.
🐢 Draw more counters to make 27.
⭐ Draw more counters to make 28.
❤ Draw more counters to make 29.
🌼 Draw more counters to make 30.

🏠 **HOME ACTIVITY** • Help your child count aloud from 1 to 30.

Ten and More

By _____

◆ **HOME ACTIVITY** • This book will help review counting on ten frames. Invite your child to share this book with you.

How many eggs? _____

© Harcourt

3

How many windows?

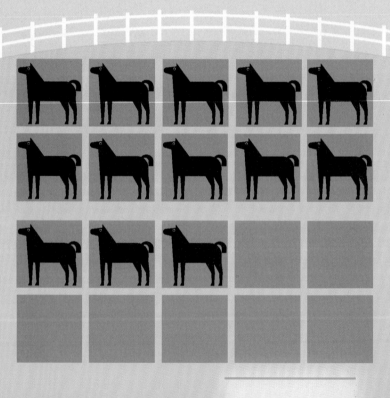

How many horses? _____

How many horseshoes? _____

How many bells? _____

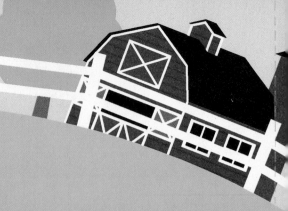

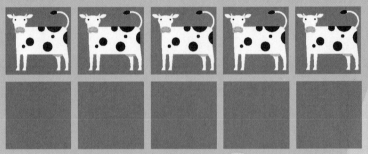

How many cows? _____

6

_____

8 **How many geese?** _____

How many sheep? _____

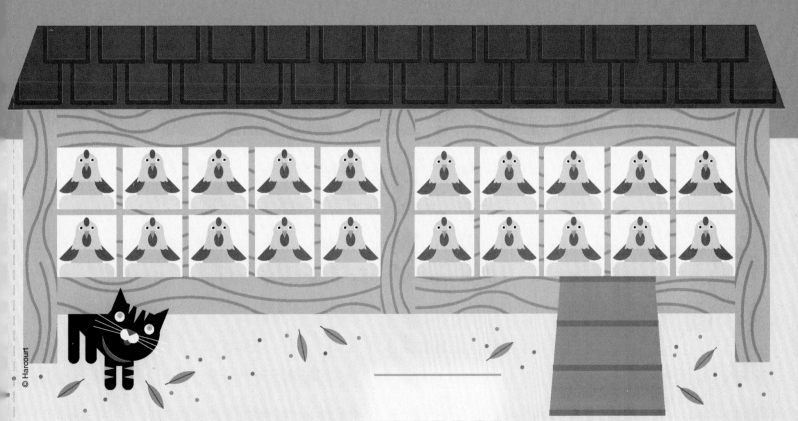

How many chickens? _____

How many hats? _____

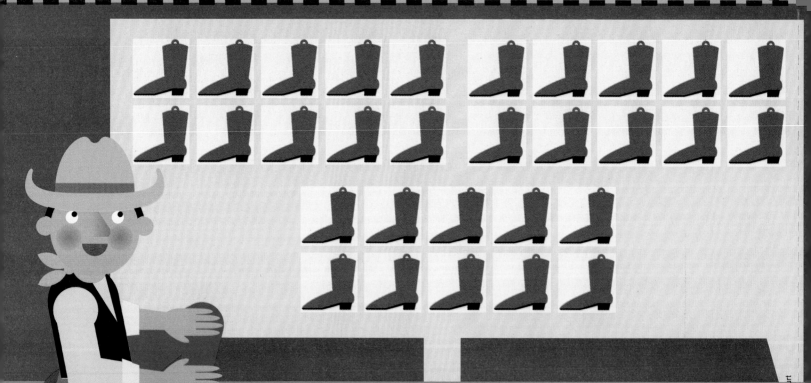

How many boots? _____

Name _____

 Review

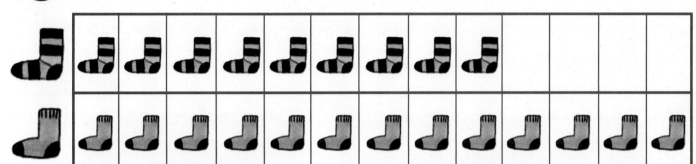

_____

_____

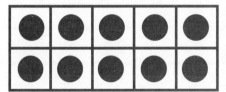  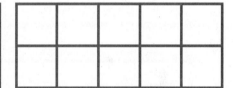

21

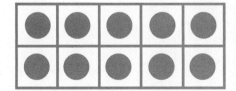  

30

Count and write how many. Circle the number that shows more.
Mark an X on the number that shows fewer.
Draw more counters to make 21.
Draw more counters to make 30.

✔ Cumulative Review

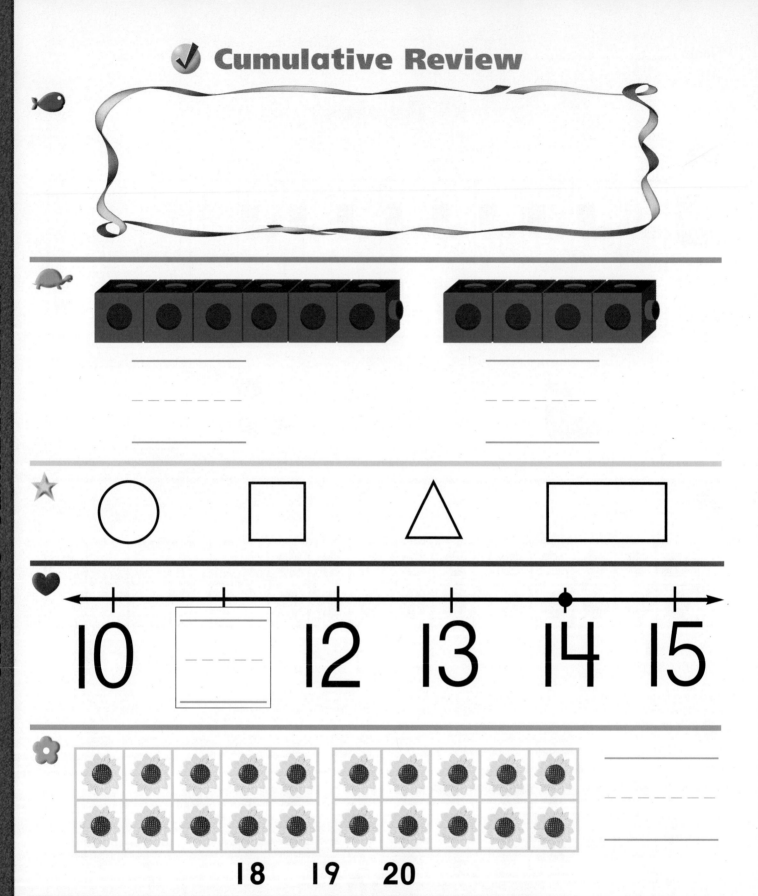

10   12   13   14   15

18   19   20

🐟 Use two colors of counters to make your own pattern. Draw your pattern.
🐢 Count the cubes. Write the numbers. Circle the number that is greater.
⭐ Circle the shape with curves. Color the shapes with four edges. Mark an X on the shape with three corners.
❤ Start at 14. Count three numbers back. Write the number.
🌼 Count the flowers. Circle the number that tells how many. Write the number.

Name _____

✔ **Test**

   13

14

     17

18

 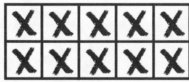    24

25

30

31

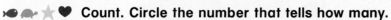

10   11   12   13   14

© Harcourt

🐟🐢⭐❤ Count. Circle the number that tells how many.
🌸 Start at 11. Count four numbers forward. Write the number.

159

CHALLENGE
Color by Number

Use these colors to color by number.

11
12
13

14
15
16

© Harcourt

Number Patterns

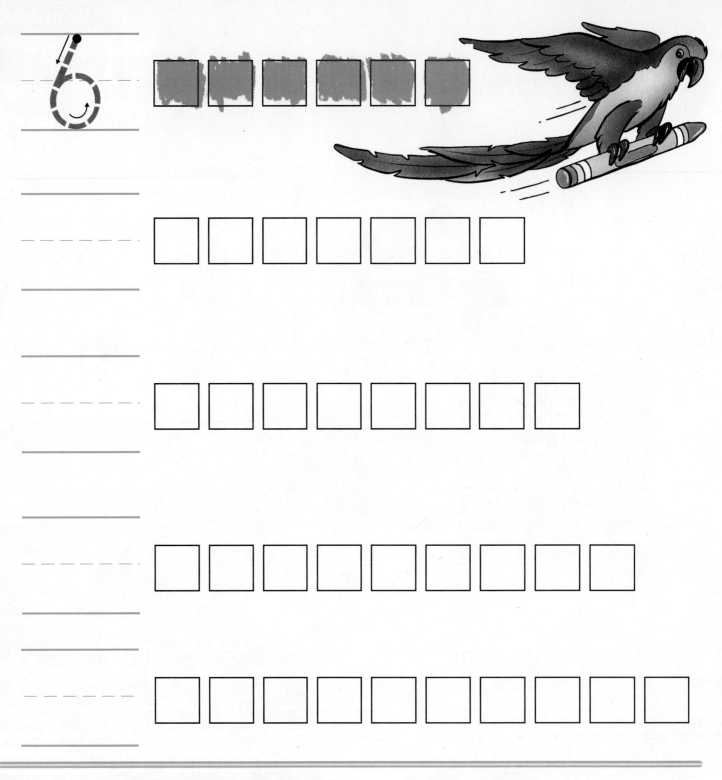

Count and color the boxes. Write the numbers.

Photography Credits:

All photography by Harcourt photographers listed, © Harcourt: Weronica Ankarorn, Victoria Bowen, Ken Kinzie, Sheri O'Neal, Quebecor Imaging, and Terry Sinclair.

Illustration Credits:

Daniel DelValle: 164; **Franklin Hammond:** Storybook; **Heidi King:** 170; **Richard Kolding:** 172; **Claude Martinot:** 165, 166, 167, 168, 169, 171, 173, 174, 177, 178, 182, 183, 184; **Stephanie Peterson:** 164; **Dorothy Stott:** 181; **Jay Veno:** 162.

© Harcourt

SCHOOL HOME CONNECTION

Dear Family,

Today we started a new chapter, *Number Patterns*. In this chapter we will learn to skip count by tens, fives, and twos. We will also learn about even and odd numbers.

Love,

_____

even

4 is an even number

An even number of cubes can be grouped in pairs.

odd

7 is an odd number

An odd number of cubes can be grouped in pairs but has one left over.

- Have your child count fingers and toes by fives and then by tens.

BOOKS TO SHARE

To read more about number patterns with your child, look for these books in your local library.

One Potato: A Counting Book of Potato Prints, by Diana Pomeroy. Harcourt, 1996.

Hundredth Day Worries, by Margery Cuyle. Simon and Schuster, 2000.

The King's Commissioners by Aileen Friedman. Scholastic, 1995.

Visit *The Learning Site* for additional ideas and activities. www.harcourtschool.com

© Harcourt

math game

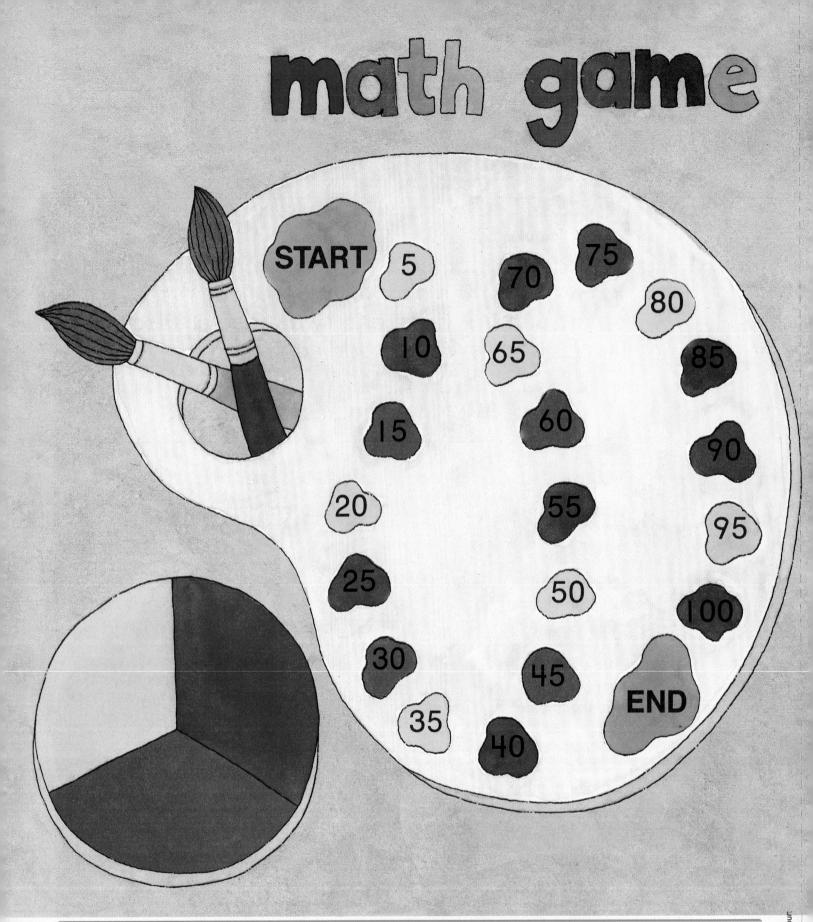

MATERIALS: 2 game markers, pencil, paper clip
DIRECTIONS: Play with a partner and decide who goes first. Put your
game marker on START. Players take turns spinning the spinner. Move your
game marker and count by fives to get to that color. The first player to get
to END wins.

1	2	3	4	5	6	7	8	9	10
11	12	13	14	15	16	17	18	19	20
21	22	23	24	25	26	27	28	29	30
31	32	33	34	35	36	37	38	39	40
41	42	43	44	45	46	47	48	49	50
51	52	53	54	55	56	57	58	59	60
61	62	63	64	65	66	67	68	69	70
71	72	73	74	75	76	77	78	79	80
81	82	83	84	85	86	87	88	89	90
91	92	93	94	95	96	97	98	99	100

© Harcourt

**Touch each number as you count from 1 to 35. Circle
each number you say. Touch and count from 36 to 68.
Circle each number you say. Touch and count from 69
to 100. Circle each number you say.**

1	2	3	4	5	6	7	8	9	10
11	12	13	14	15	16	17	18	19	20
21	22	23	24	25	26	27	28	29	30
31	32	33	34	35	36	37	38	39	40
41	42	43	44	45	46	47	48	49	50
51	52	53	54	55	56	57	58	59	60
61	62	63	64	65	66	67	68	69	70
71	72	73	74	75	76	77	78	79	80
81	82	83	84	85	86	87	88	89	90
91	92	93	94	95	96	97	98	99	100

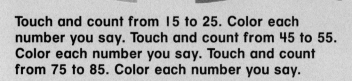
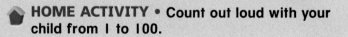

Touch and count from 15 to 25. Color each number you say. Touch and count from 45 to 55. Color each number you say. Touch and count from 75 to 85. Color each number you say.

⬠ **HOME ACTIVITY** • Count out loud with your child from 1 to 100.

166

1	2	3	4	5	6	7	8	9	10
11	12	13	14	15	16	17	18	19	20
21	22	23	24	25	26	27	28	29	30
31	32	33	34	35	36	37	38	39	40
41	42	43	44	45	46	47	48	49	50
51	52	53	54	55	56	57	58	59	60
61	62	63	64	65	66	67	68	69	70
71	72	73	74	75	76	77	78	79	80
81	82	83	84	85	86	87	88	89	90
91	92	93	94	95	96	97	98	99	100

© Harcourt

Touch and count by tens. Use blue to color the
numbers you say.

1	2	3	4	5	6	7	8	9	1⓪
11	12	13	14	15	16	17	18	19	2⓪
21	22	23	24	25	26	27	28	29	3⓪
31	32	33	34	35	36	37	38	39	4⓪
41	42	43	44	45	46	47	48	49	5⓪
51	52	53	54	55	56	57	58	59	6⓪
61	62	63	64	65	66	67	68	69	7⓪
71	72	73	74	75	76	77	78	79	8⓪
81	82	83	84	85	86	87	88	89	9⓪
91	92	93	94	95	96	97	98	99	10⓪

Touch and count by tens. Finish writing the numbers.

HOME ACTIVITY • Help your child count by tens to 100.

1	2	3	4	5	6	7	8	9	10
11	12	13	14	15	16	17	18	19	20
21	22	23	24	25	26	27	28	29	30
31	32	33	34	35	36	37	38	39	40
41	42	43	44	45	46	47	48	49	50
51	52	53	54	55	56	57	58	59	60
61	62	63	64	65	66	67	68	69	70
71	72	73	74	75	76	77	78	79	80
81	82	83	84	85	86	87	88	89	90
91	92	93	94	95	96	97	98	99	100

Put a red cube on each number that ends with a 5 or a 0.
Color these boxes red. Touch and count by fives.

5   10   15   20   25

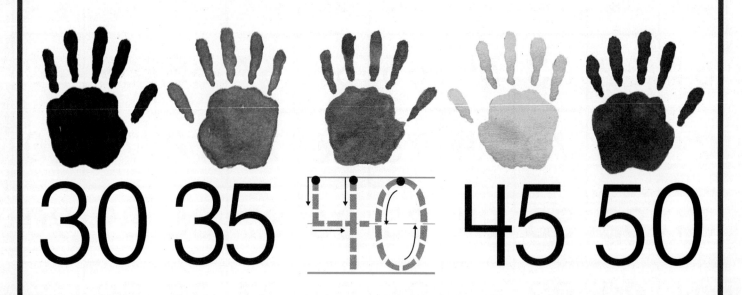

30 35 40 45 50

Put 5 connecting cubes above each hand. Count by fives. Trace the numbers.

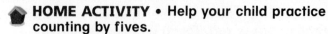 **HOME ACTIVITY** • Help your child practice counting by fives.

170

1	2	3	4	5	6	7	8	9	10
11	12	13	14	15	16	17	18	19	20
21	22	23	24	25	26	27	28	29	30
31	32	33	34	35	36	37	38	39	40
41	42	43	44	45	46	47	48	49	50
51	52	53	54	55	56	57	58	59	60
61	62	63	64	65	66	67	68	69	70
71	72	73	74	75	76	77	78	79	80
81	82	83	84	85	86	87	88	89	90
91	92	93	94	95	96	97	98	99	100

Put a yellow cube on the 2, 4, 6, 8, 10, 12, and 14.
Color these boxes yellow. Color to finish the pattern.
Touch and count by twos.

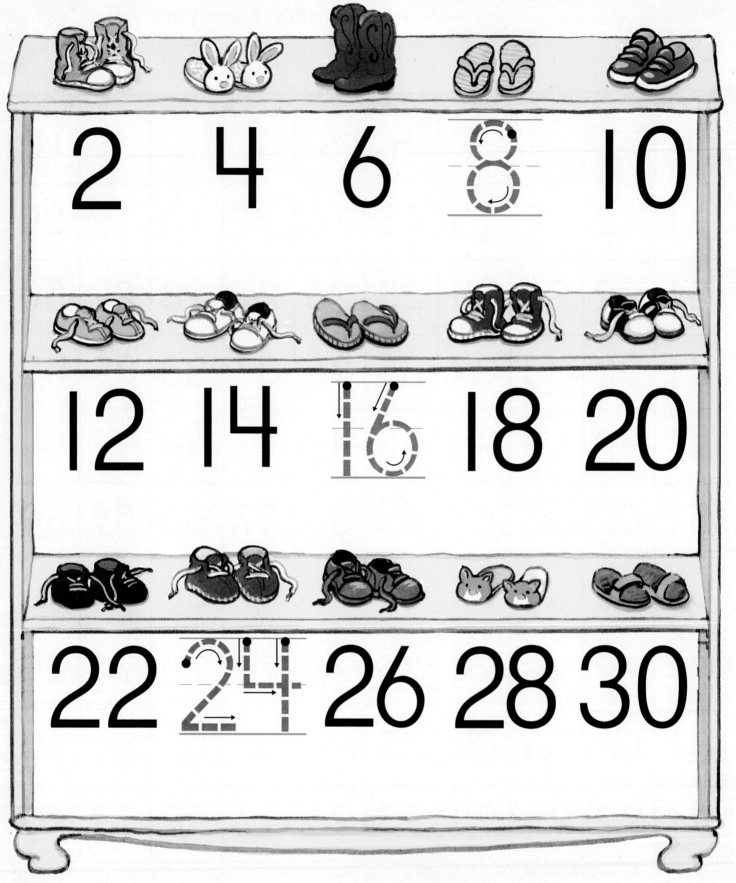

Count by twos. Trace the numbers.

HOME ACTIVITY • Give your child a handful of pennies. Have him or her group the pennies in pairs and then count them by twos.

172

Name _____

Problem Solving Strategy
Find a Pattern

1	2	3	4	5	6	7	8	9	10
11	12	13	14	15	16	17	18	19	20
21	22	23	24	25	26	27	28	29	30
31	32	33	34	35	36	37	38	39	40
41	42	43	44	45	46	47	48	49	50
51	52	53	54	55	56	57	58	59	60
61	62	63	64	65	66	67	68	69	70
71	72	73	74	75	76	77	78	79	80
81	82	83	84	85	86	87	88	89	90
91	92	93	94	95	96	97	98	99	100

PROBLEM SOLVING

Use yellow to color the numbers you say when you count by fives. Use blue to circle the numbers you say when you count by tens. What patterns do you see?

© Harcourt

173

1	2	3	4	5	6	7	8	9	10
11	12	13	14	15	16	17	18	19	20
21	22	23	24	25	26	27	28	29	30
31	32	33	34	35	36	37	38	39	40
41	42	43	44	45	46	47	48	49	50
51	52	53	54	55	56	57	58	59	60
61	62	63	64	65	66	67	68	69	70
71	72	73	74	75	76	77	78	79	80
81	82	83	84	85	86	87	88	89	90
91	92	93	94	95	96	97	98	99	100

Use yellow to color the numbers you say when you count by twos. Use red to color the other numbers. What pattern do you see?

HOME ACTIVITY • Encourage your child to count by ones, twos, fives, and tens while you shop, walk, or ride together.

Name _____

✔️ **Review**

1	2	3	4	5	6	7	8	9	10
11	12	13	14	15	16	17	18	19	20
21	22	23	24	25	26	27	28	29	30
31	32	33	34	35	36	37	38	39	40
41	42	43	44	45	46	47	48	49	50
51	52	53	54	55	56	57	58	59	60
61	62	63	64	65	66	67	68	69	70
71	72	73	74	75	76	77	78	79	80
81	82	83	84	85	86	87	88	89	90
91	92	93	94	95	96	97	98	99	100

Touch and count by tens. Finish writing the numbers. Use blue to circle the numbers you say. Touch and count by fives. Use green to color the numbers you say.

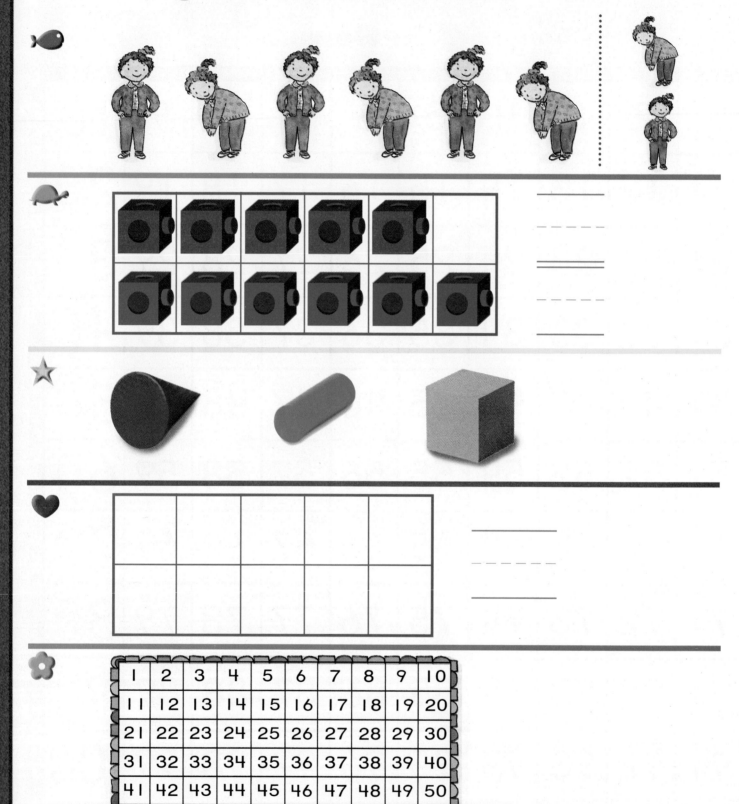

1	2	3	4	5	6	7	8	9	10
11	12	13	14	15	16	17	18	19	20
21	22	23	24	25	26	27	28	29	30
31	32	33	34	35	36	37	38	39	40
41	42	43	44	45	46	47	48	49	50

🐟 Circle what you would most likely do next.
🐢 Count the cubes in each row and write the number. Circle the number that is greater.
⭐ Circle the shapes that stack and slide.
❤️ Draw counters in the ten frame to show the number that is two more than eight.
Write the number.
🌼 Touch and count by tens. Use blue to color the numbers you say.

© Harcourt

176

20

40

30

10

50

0

60

100

70

90

80

Count by tens to connect the dots in order.

© Harcourt

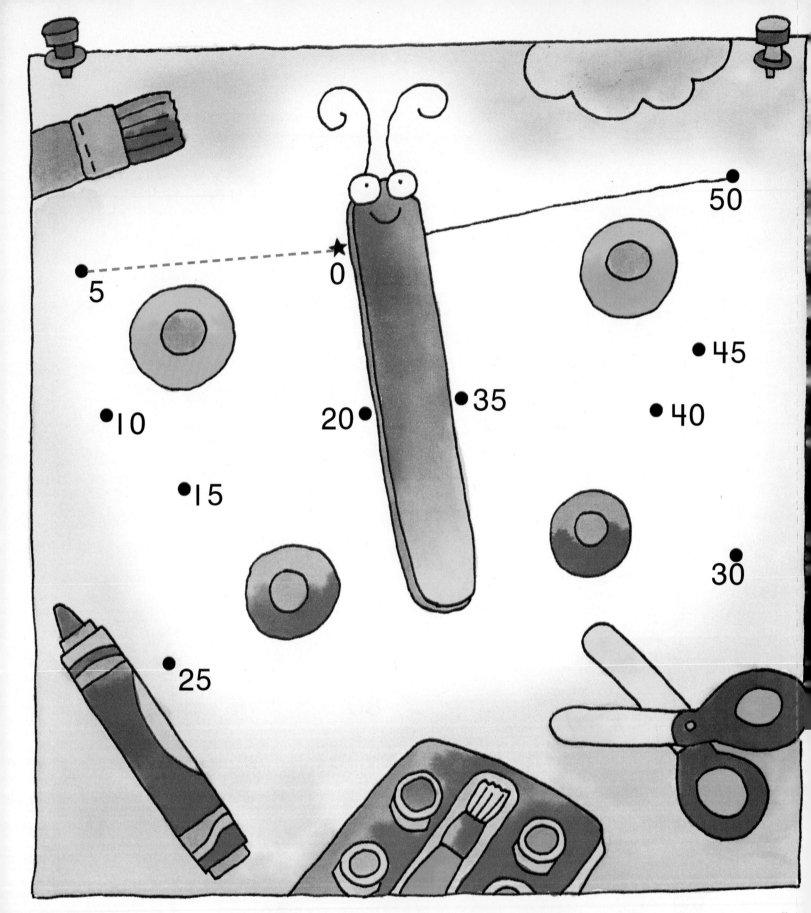

Count by fives to connect the dots in order.

HOME ACTIVITY • Have your child show you how he or she counted by fives to connect the dots.

 **Build the cube train. Take one cube from each
end of the train and snap these cubes together. Do this as
many times as you can. If you have only pairs, the number
is even. Circle the number. If you have one cube left over,
the number is odd. Mark an X on the number.**

7

8

★

9

10

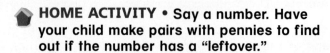 ★ ♥ Build the cube train. Take one cube from each end of the train and snap these cubes together. Do this as many times as you can. If you have only pairs, the number is even. Circle the number. If you have one cube left over, the number is odd. Mark an X on the number.

HOME ACTIVITY • Say a number. Have your child make pairs with pennies to find out if the number has a "leftover."

Name _____

 Ordinal Numbers

 Circle the fifth child. Draw a line under the seventh child. Mark an X on the tenth child.

 Circle the first bear. Draw a line under the sixth bear. Mark an X on the ninth bear.

181

© Harcourt

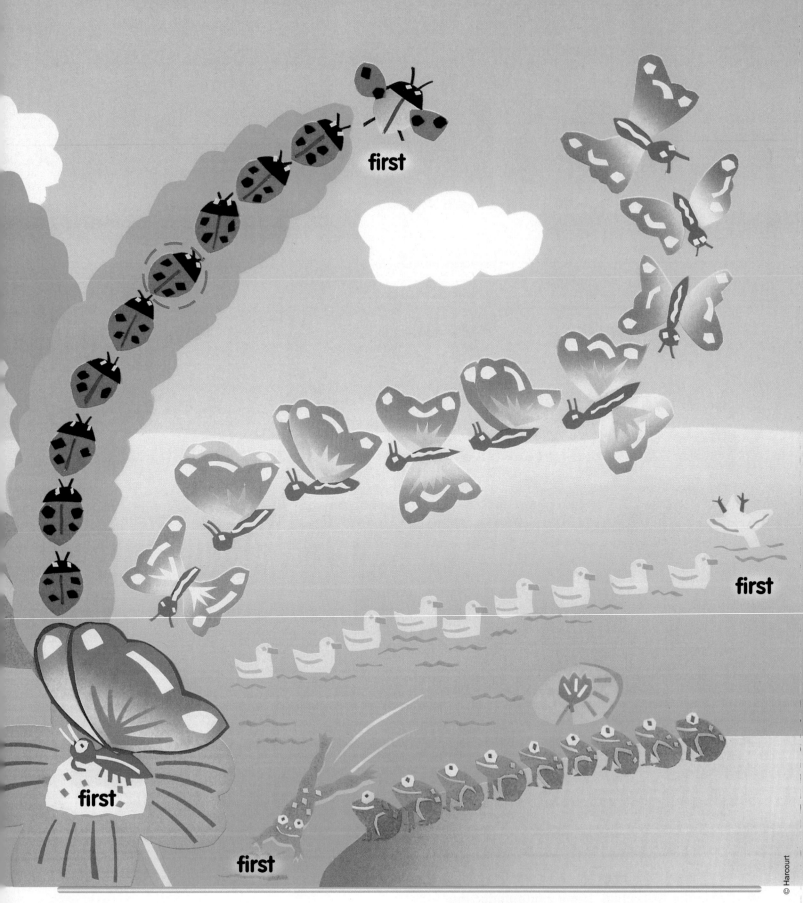

first

first

first

first

Circle the fifth ladybug. Circle the second butterfly. Circle the seventh duck. Circle the ninth frog.

🏠 **HOME ACTIVITY** • Have your child use position words such as *first* and *third* to tell the order of the animals in each line.

182

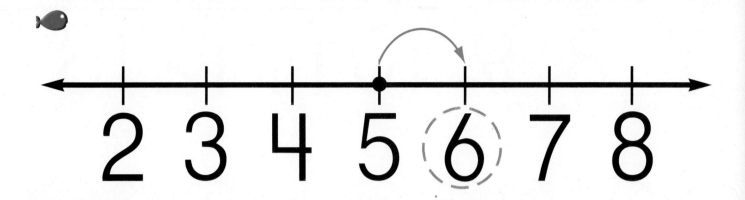

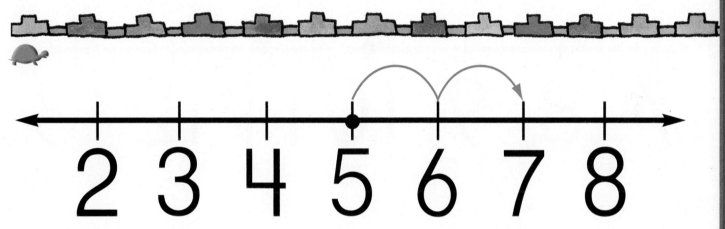

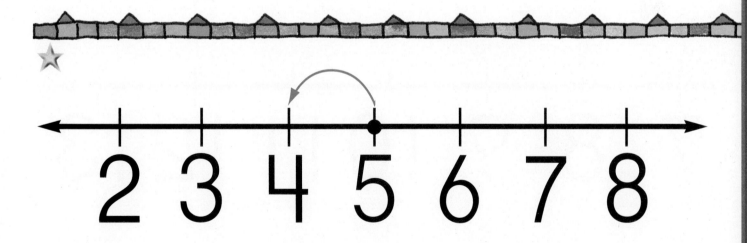

PROBLEM SOLVING

🐟 **Put your finger on 5. Count up 1. What number are you on? Circle the number.**

🐢 **Put your finger on 5. Count up 2. What number are you on? Circle the number.**

⭐ **Put your finger on 5. Count back 1. What number are you on? Circle the number.**

183

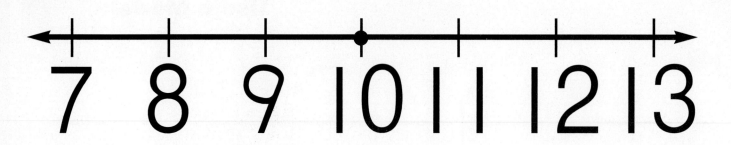

7 8 9 10 11 12 13

7 8 9 10 11 12 13

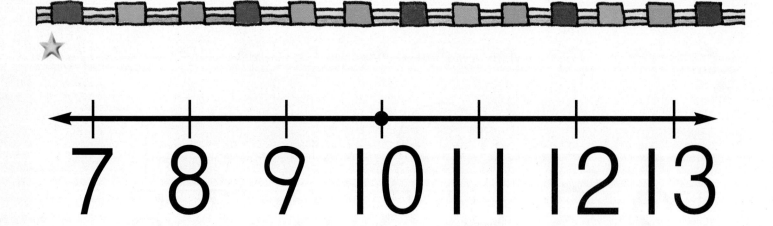

7 8 9 10 11 12 13

🐟 Put your finger on 10. Count back 1.
What number are you on? Circle the number.
🐟 Put your finger on 10. Count back 2.
What number are you on? Circle the number.
⭐ Put your finger on 10. Count up 1. What
number are you on? Circle the number.

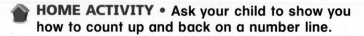 **HOME ACTIVITY** • Ask your child to show you
how to count up and back on a number line.

Counting Is Fun

2

5

10

By _____

⬠ **HOME ACTIVITY** • This book will help review skip-counting. Invite your child to share this book with you.

1

© Harcourt

2 4 6 8 10

3

2 4 6 8 10

Let's count by twos.

2

5 10 15 20 25

Let's count by fives.

4

10 20

30 40 50

Let's count by tens.

2 4 6 8 10

5 10 15 20 25

10 20 30 40 50

Let's count by twos, fives, and tens.

8

Name _____

✅ **Review**

5

first

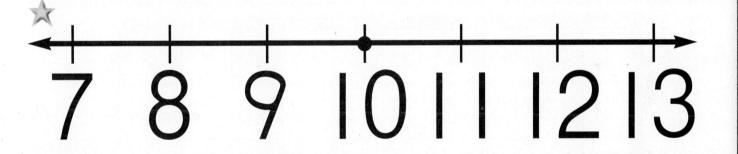

7 8 9 10 11 12 13

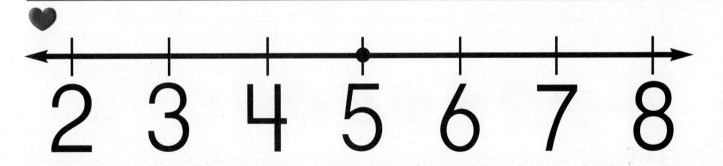

2 3 4 5 6 7 8

🐟 Build the cube train. Take a cube from each end of the train and snap these cubes together.
Do this as many times as you can. If you have only pairs, the number is even. Circle the number.
If you have one cube left over, the number is odd. Mark an X on the number.
🐢 Circle the seventh child.
⭐ Put your finger on 10. Count up 1. What number are you on? Circle the number.
❤ Put your finger on 5. Count back 1. What number are you on? Circle the number.

✔ Cumulative Review

1	2	3	4	5	6	7	8	9	10
11	12	13	14	15	16	17	18	19	20
21	22	23	24	25	26	27	28	29	30

first

🐟 Circle the fish that is in the fishbowl.

🐢 Circle the bird that is over the tree.

⭐ Use counters to show the same pattern. Draw the pattern.

❤ Look at the object at the beginning of the row. Color in the outline that matches the shape of the object.

🌼 Color to continue the pattern. Touch and count by twos.

🦋 Circle the fifth ladybug. Draw a line under the seventh ladybug. Mark an X on the tenth ladybug.

186

Name _____

✔️ Test

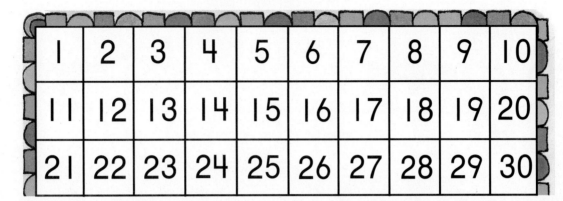

1	2	3	4	5	6	7	8	9	10
11	12	13	14	15	16	17	18	19	20
21	22	23	24	25	26	27	28	29	30

7

first

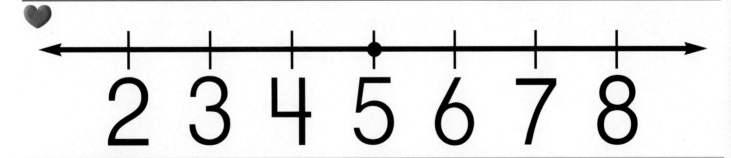

2 3 4 5 6 7 8

🐟 Use green to color the numbers you say when you count by fives.

🐠 Build the cube train. Take one cube from each end of the train and snap these cubes together. Do this as many times as you can. If you have only pairs, the number is even. Circle the number. If you have one cube left over the number is odd. Mark an X on the number.

⭐ Circle the tenth child.

❤️ Put your finger on 5. Count up 2. What number are you on? Circle the number.

CHALLENGE
Counting on the Calculator

0 1 2 3 ___ ___ ___

0 ___ 2 4 6 ___ ___ ___

 Use a calculator. Press [ON/C] [0] [+] [1] [=] . Now, keep pressing [=] .
Write the missing numbers. What number pattern do you see?

Use a calculator. Press [ON/C] [0] [+] [2] [=] . Now, keep pressing [=] .
Write the missing numbers. What number pattern do you see?

Money and Time

BUG BANK

Draw a line to match the front of each coin to its back.

Photography Credits:

All photography by Harcourt photographers listed, © Harcourt: Weronica Ankarorn, Victoria Bowen, Ken Kinzie, Sheri O'Neal, Quebecor Imaging, and Terry Sinclair.

Illustration Credits:

Liz Allen: 207, 208; **Russel Bencati:** 193; **Ken Bowser:** 198; **Susan Calitri:** 199, 200; **Carolyn Croll:** Storybook; **Obadinah Heavner:** 205; **C.D. Hullinger:** cvr, 190; **Judy Love:** 203, 204; **Claude Martinot:** 192; **Peggy Tagel:** 194; **Sally Vitsky:** 206.

© Harcourt

SCHOOL HOME

CONNECTION

Dear Family,

Today we started a new chapter, Money and Time. We will learn to recognize coins and their value. We will also learn about time, using a calendar and a clock.

Love,

_____

Heads   Tails

 penny

 nickel

 dime

ACTIVITY

• Have your child sort a handful of change so that all the coins that are alike are together.

• Choose a "coin of the day," and talk about what is shown on both sides of the coin.

BOOKS TO SHARE

To read about money with your child, look for these books at your local library.

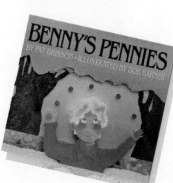

Benny's Pennies, by Pat Brisson. Yearling, 1993.

26 Letters and 99 Cents, by Tana Hoban. Morrow, 1995.

Jelly Beans for Sale, by Bruce McMillan. Scholastic, 1996.

 Visit *The Learning Site* for additional ideas and activities. www.harcourtschool.com

MATERIALS: number cube (1–6), game marker for each player
DIRECTIONS: Players take turns tossing the number cube and moving their game marker that number of spaces. Players are to name the coin and tell its value. If a player lands on a flower with a coin, he or she should tell how many pennies the coin is worth. The first player to get to the wishing well wins.

Name _____

 **or**

I ¢

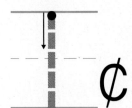 **I ¢**

_____ **¢**

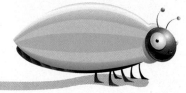

_____ **¢**

_____ **¢**

   **Count the pennies.
Write how many cents.**

193

 ¢

_____ ¢

_____

_____ ¢

_____ ¢

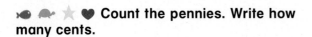 Count the pennies. Write how many cents.

🏠 **HOME ACTIVITY** • Place a handful of coins on a table. Ask your child to sort out the pennies, count them, and tell you how many cents there are.

Name _____

10¢

or

10¢

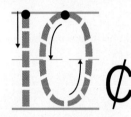

_____ ¢

_____ ¢

_____ ¢

_____ ¢

 Write how many cents. Circle the coins that show 10¢.

10 ¢

_____ ¢

_____ _____ ¢

_____ _____ ¢

_____ _____ ¢

_____ _____ ¢

🐟 🐢 ⭐ 💙🌸🦋 Write how many cents. Circle the coins that show 10¢.

🏠 **HOME ACTIVITY** • Using 10 pennies, 1 nickel, and 1 dime, ask your child to sort the coins and tell how many cents are in each group.

198

© Harcourt

Name _____

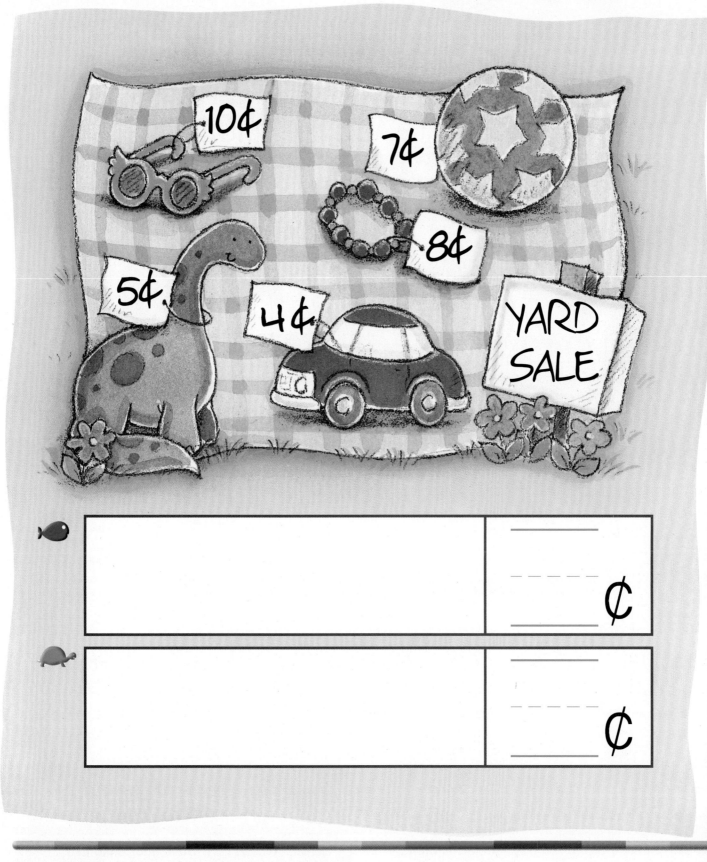

PROBLEM SOLVING

Choose a toy to buy. Circle the toy. Then draw the coins you would use to buy it. Write how many cents.

199

PLANT SALE

5¢ 10¢ 10¢ 2¢ 8¢ 4¢

_____ ¢

_____ ¢

Choose a plant to buy. Circle the plant. Then draw the coins you would use to buy it. Write how many cents.

 **HOME ACTIVITY** • Have your child use pennies, nickels, and dimes to practice "buying" objects in your home.

Name _____

✔️ Review

_____ ¢

_____ ¢

_____ ¢

_____ ¢

_____ ¢

🐟 **Count the pennies. Write how many cents.**
🐢⭐ **Write how many cents. Circle the coins that show 5¢.**
❤️🌸 **Write how many cents. Circle the coins that show 10¢.**

✓ Cumulative Review

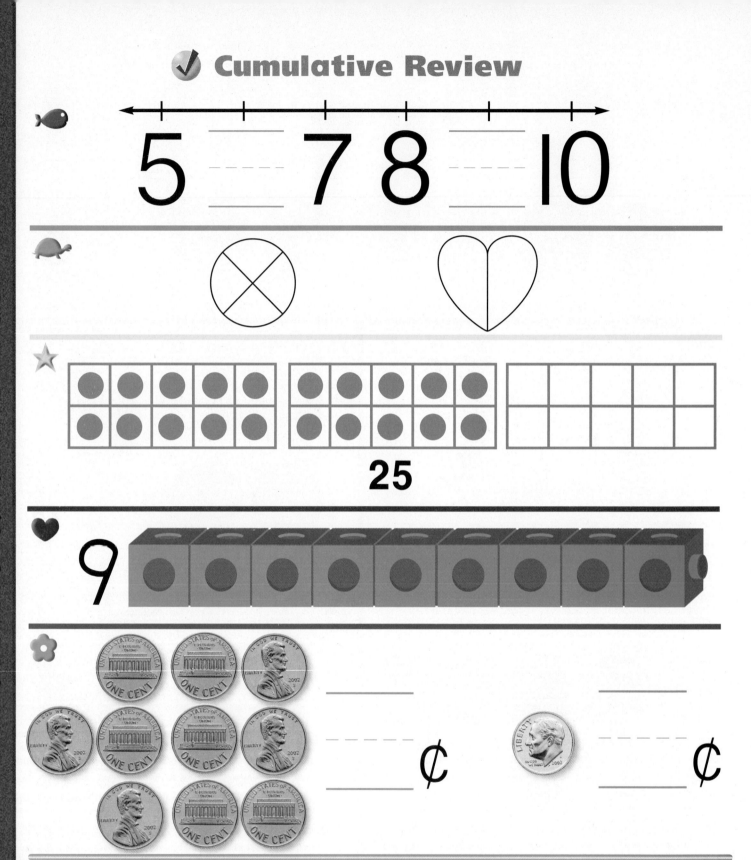

5 ___ ___ 7 8 ___ 10

25

9

___ ¢   ___ ¢

🐟 Write the number that is after 5. Write the number that is before 10.

🐢 Use green to color one part of each shape. Use red to circle the shape that shows one half. Use blue to circle the shape that shows one fourth.

⭐ Draw more counters to make 25.

💙 Build the cube train. Take one cube from each end of the train and snap these cubes together. Do this as many times as you can. If you have only pairs, the number is even. Circle the number. If you have one cube left over, the number is odd. Mark an X on the number.

🌸 Write how many cents.

Morning, Afternoon, Evening

What times of day do the pictures show?
Circle the time of day that is missing.

What times of day do the pictures show? Circle the time of day that is missing.

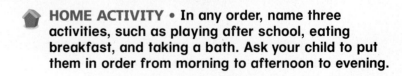

HOME ACTIVITY • In any order, name three activities, such as playing after school, eating breakfast, and taking a bath. Ask your child to put them in order from morning to afternoon to evening.

March

Sunday	Monday	Tuesday	Wednesday	Thursday	Friday	Saturday
	1	2	3	4	5	6
7	8	9	10	11	12	13
14	15	16	17	18	19	20
21	22	23	24	25	26	27
28	29	30	31			

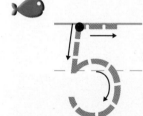 **Wednesdays**

 _____ **Fridays**

 _____ **Saturdays**

 _____ **Days in March**

🐟 Count the Wednesdays. Write how many.
🐢 Count the Fridays. Write how many.
⭐ Count the Saturdays. Write how many.
❤ Write how many days in March.

PROBLEM SOLVING

205

April

Sunday	Monday	Tuesday	Wednesday	Thursday	Friday	Saturday
				1	2	3
4	5		7	8	9	10
	12	13	14	15		17
18	19	20		22	23	24
	26	27	28	29	30	

Trace the numbers and fill in the missing numbers.
Circle the name of the month.
Color the first day of the month green.
Color the last day of the month red.

HOME ACTIVITY • Show your child the calendar page for this month. Help him or her find and name today's day and date.

© Harcourt

206

Name _____

More Time, Less Time

    Circle the activity that takes more time.

 Circle the activity that takes less time.

 HOME ACTIVITY • Have your child predict which of two chores will take more time. Then have him or her act out the chores to see which took longer.

208

Name _____

3 o'clock

3:00

3 o'clock

Write the numbers on the clock. Circle the number that tells where the hour hand is pointing.

© Harcourt

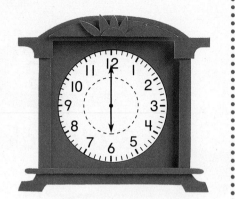

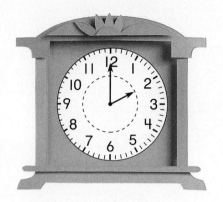

 6 o'clock

_____ o'clock

_____ o'clock

_____ o'clock

_____ o'clock

_____ o'clock

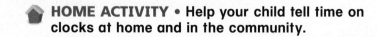

Write the number that tells the hour. Circle the two clocks that show the same time.

HOME ACTIVITY • Help your child tell time on clocks at home and in the community.

210

© Harcourt

Look What I Found!

By _____

HOME ACTIVITY • This book will help review money and days of the week. Invite your child to share this book with you.

I

Look what I found! _____ _____ ¢

3

**On Monday
I went with Grandpa.**

2

**On Tuesday
I went with Mom.**

4

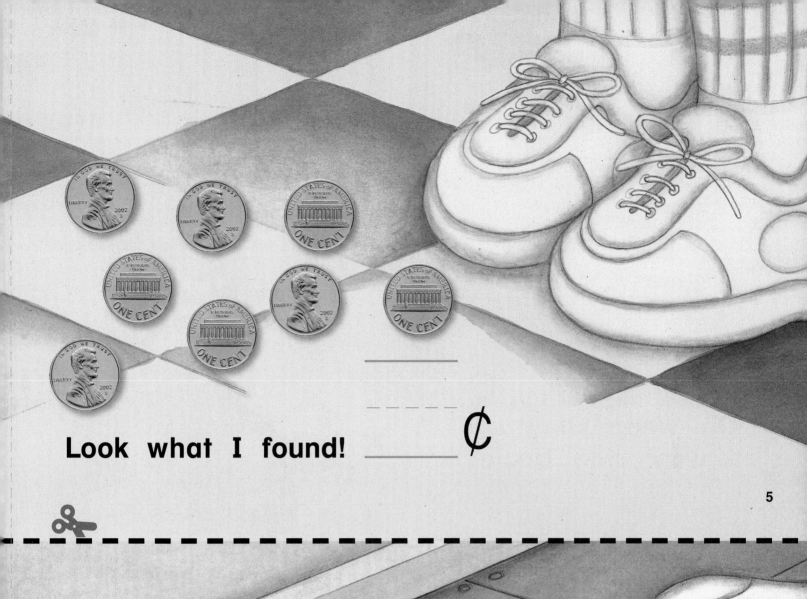

Look what I found! _____ ¢

Look what I found! _____ ¢

On Wednesday
I went with Uncle Gary.

6

On Thursday
I went with Nana.

8

Look what I found! _____ ¢

9

Look what I found! _____ ¢

11

On Friday
I went with Mango.

10

On Saturday
I went shopping.

12

Name _____

✔ Review

March

Sunday	Monday	Tuesday	Wednesday	Thursday	Friday	Saturday
	1	2	3	4	5	6
7	8	9	10	11	12	13
14	15	16	17	18	19	20
21	22	23	24	25	26	27
28	29	30	31			

 _____

_ _ _ _ _ _ _

_____ **Wednesdays**

 _____

_ _ _ _ _ _ _

_____ **Fridays**

What times of day do the pictures show? Circle the time of day that is missing.

🐢 Count the Wednesdays. Write how many.

⭐ Count the Fridays. Write how many.

❤ Circle the activity that takes more time.

211

✔ Cumulative Review

  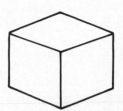 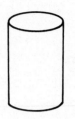

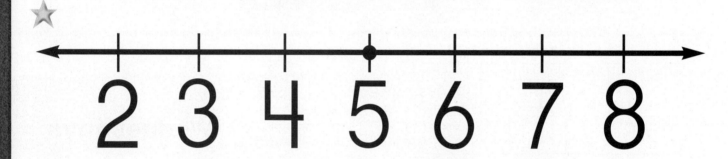

2 3 4 5 6 7 8

  ¢     ¢

 Use blue to color the cylinder. Use red to color the sphere. Use yellow to color the cube.
Use green to color the cone.
🐢 Use green to circle the shape with curves. Use purple to circle the shapes with four sides.
Use orange to circle the shape with three corners.
⭐ Put your finger on 5. Count up 2. What number are you on? Circle the number.
❤ Write how many cents. Circle the coins that show 5¢.
 Circle the activity that takes more time.

Name _____

  _____ ¢   _____ ¢

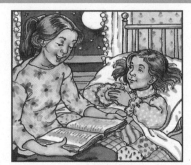 

March

Sunday	Monday	Tuesday	Wednesday	Thursday	Friday	Saturday
	1	2	3	4	5	6
7	8	9	10	11	12	13
14	15	16	17	18	19	20
21	22	23	24	25	26	27
28	29	30	31			

 _____ **Saturdays**

 _____ **Days in March**

🐟 Write how many cents.
🐢 What times of day do the pictures show? Circle the time of day that is missing.
⭐ Count the Saturdays. Write how many.
❤ Write how many days in March.
🌸 Circle the activity that takes less time.

CHALLENGE

Dimes and Nickels

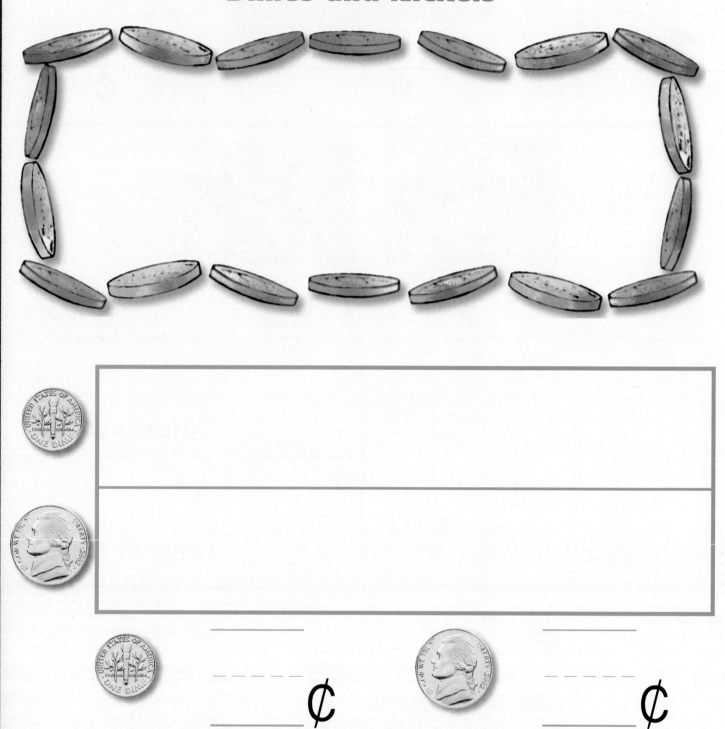

_____ ¢   _____ ¢

Place a handful of dimes and nickels on the workspace. Sort the coins by kind. Move the coins to the box. Count the dimes by tens, write how many cents. Count the nickels by fives. Write how many cents. Circle the amount that shows the greater value.

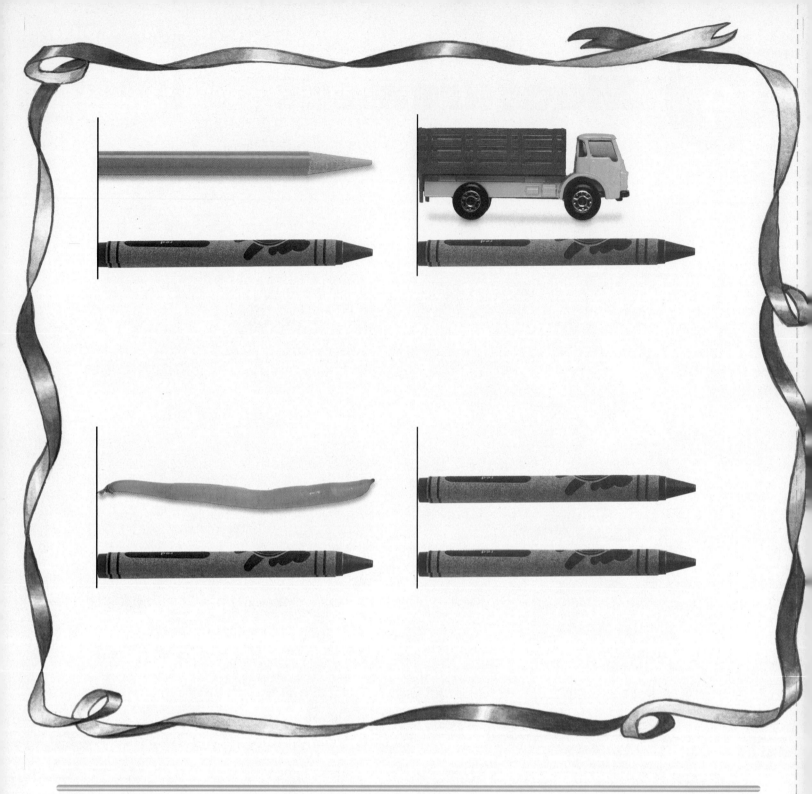

Circle the objects that are about as long as one red crayon.

Copyright © by Harcourt, Inc.
2007 Edition

All rights reserved. No part of this publication may be reproduced or transmitted in any form or by any means, electronic or mechanical, including photocopy, recording, or any information storage and retrieval system, without permission in writing from the publisher.

Requests for permission to make copies of any part of the work should be addressed to School Permissions and Copyrights, Harcourt, Inc., 6277 Sea Harbor Drive, Orlando, Florida 32887-6777. Fax: 407-345-2418.

HARCOURT and the Harcourt Logo are trademarks of Harcourt, Inc., registered in the United States of America and/or other jurisdictions.

Grateful acknowledgment is made to Troll Communications L. L. C. for permission to reprint the cover illustration by Cheryl Nathan from *The Long and Short of It* by Cheryl Nathan and Lisa McCourt. Illustration copyright © 1998 by Cheryl Nathan.

Printed in the United States of America

216

Photography Credits:

All photography by Harcourt photographers listed, © Harcourt: Weronica Ankarorn, Victoria Bowen, Ken Kinzie, Sheri O'Neal, Quebecor Imaging, and Terry Sinclair.

Illustration Credits:

Shirley Beckes: 221, 222; **Rose Mary Berlin:** 215, 218; **Nan Brooks:** 235, 236; **Shelley Dieterichs:** 223, 224, storybook; **Judy Love:** 231, 232; **Stephanie Peterson:** 225, 226.

© Harcourt

SCHOOL HOME CONNECTION

Dear Family,

Today we started a new chapter, Measurement. We will learn to measure how long objects are. We will also compare how much different containers hold and how heavy different objects are.

Love,

_____

Vocabulary Power

shortest, longest

The bow is the shortest. The toothbrush is the longest.

ACTIVITY

- Help your child compare an earlier height measurement with his or her height today.

- Have your child compare the amounts of water two different plastic containers hold.

BOOKS TO SHARE

To read about measurement with your child, look for these books at your local library.

The Long and Short of It, by Cheryl Nathan and Lisa McCourt. Bridge-water Books, 1998.

Inch by Inch, by Leo Lionni. Morrow, 1995.

Twice My Size, by Adrian Mitchell. Millbrook, 1999.

 GO ON-LINE Visit *The Learning Site* for additional ideas and activities. www.harcourtschool.com

MATH GAME

MATERIALS: classroom book, paper clip, pencil

DIRECTIONS: Play with a partner and decide who goes first. Players take turns spinning the spinner and finding objects that are longer than, shorter than, wider than, taller than, thicker than, or thinner than a book. The first player to use all sections of the spinner wins.

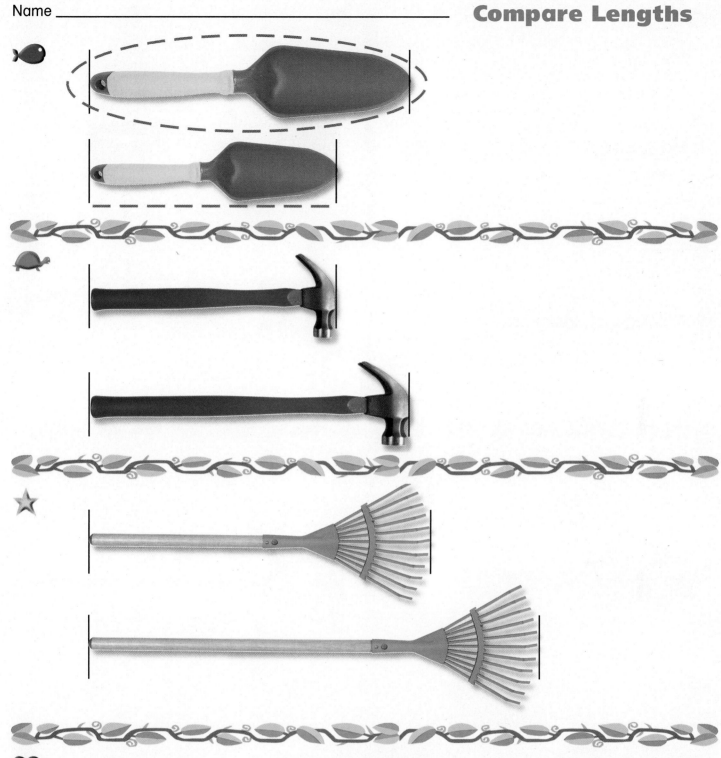

Circle the longer object. Draw a line under the shorter object.

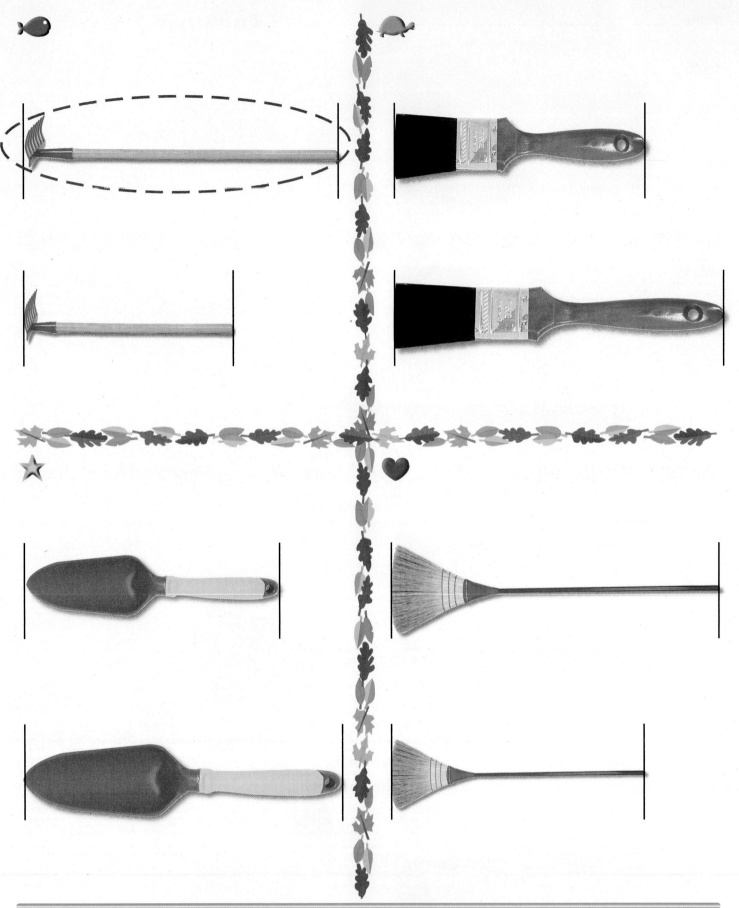

🐟 🐢 ⭐ ❤️ Circle the longer object. Draw a line under the shorter object.

⬠ **HOME ACTIVITY** • Have your child compare the lengths of a fork and a spoon and tell which is longer.

220

Order Lengths

🐟 🐢 ⭐ ♥ **Circle the groups of objects that are in order from shortest to longest, starting at the top.**

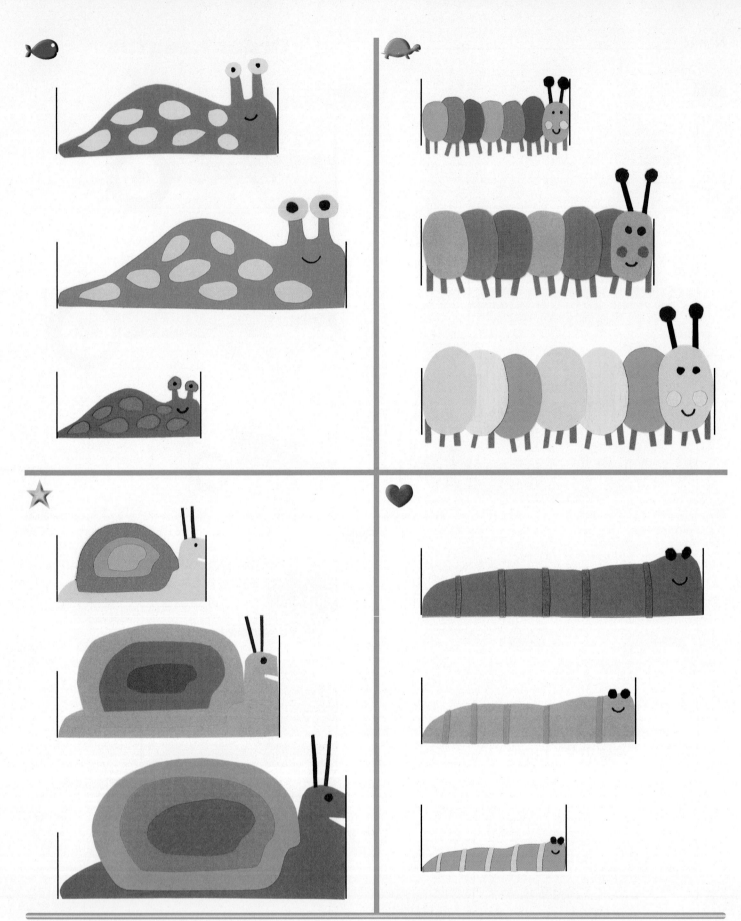

🐟 🐢 ⭐ ♥ Circle the groups of objects that are in order from shortest to longest, starting at the top.

🏠 **HOME ACTIVITY** • Have your child put a teaspoon, a tablespoon, and a serving spoon in order from shortest to longest.

222

HANDS ON

Go on a measurement walk. Use yarn of different colors to measure the counter and the door. Cut the yarn and compare the two pieces. Circle the picture of the place where you used the longer piece.

Use yarn of different colors to measure the desk and the shelves. Cut the yarn and compare the two pieces. Circle the picture of the place where you used the longer piece.

 Go on a measurement walk. Use yarn of different colors to measure the table and the bulletin board. Cut the yarn and compare the two pieces. Circle the picture of the place where you used the shorter piece.

Use yarn of different colors to measure the easel and the chair. Cut the yarn and compare the two pieces. Circle the picture of the place where you used the shorter piece.

224

4 **cubes**

_____ **cubes**

_____ **cubes**

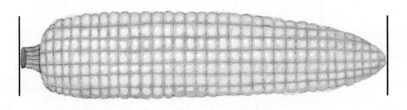

_____ **cubes**

Use cubes to measure the vegetable. About
how many cubes long is it? Write the number.

225

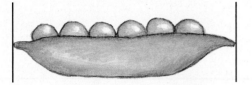

 **cubes**

_____
- - - - -
_____ **cubes**

_____
- - - - -
_____ **cubes**

_____
- - - - -
_____ **cubes**

 Use cubes to measure the vegetable. About how many cubes long is it? Write the number.

HOME ACTIVITY • Have your child show you how he or she placed the cubes to measure the objects on this page.

Name _____

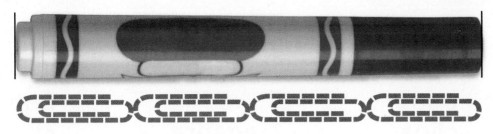

_____
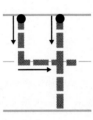
Estimate _____ paper clips   **Measure** _____ paper clips

_____   _____
Estimate _____ paper clips   **Measure** _____ paper clips

_____   _____
Estimate _____ paper clips   **Measure** _____ paper clips

PROBLEM SOLVING

Estimate about how many paper clips long the object
is. Then measure. Write about how many paper clips long it is.

© Harcourt

Estimate _____ **paper clips**   Measure _____ **paper clips**

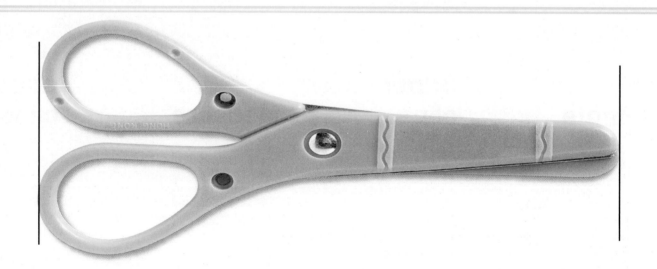

Estimate _____ **paper clips**   Measure _____ **paper clips**

Estimate about how many paper clips long the object is. Then measure. Write about how many paper clips long it is.

HOME ACTIVITY • Have your child estimate the lengths of objects in paper clips and then measure them to check.

228

© Harcourt

Name _____

✅ Review

_____
_____ **cubes**

_____
Estimate _____ **paper clips**   **Measure** _____ **paper clips**

🐟 Circle the longer object. Underline the shorter object.
🐢 Use yarn in different colors to measure the teacher's desk and your table. Cut the yarn and compare the two pieces. Circle the picture of the place where you used the longer piece.
⭐ Use cubes to measure the carrot. Write the number that tells about how many cubes long it is.
♥ Estimate about how many paper clips long the crayon is. Then measure. Write about how many paper clips long it is.

229

Cumulative Review

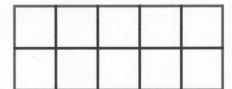

16

X	X	X	X	X
X	X	X	X	X

_____

_____ ¢

March

Sunday	Monday	Tuesday	Wednesday	Thursday	Friday	Saturday
	1	2	3	4	5	6
7	8	9	10	11	12	13
14	15	16	17	18	19	20
21	22	23	24	25	26	27
28	29	30	31			

_____ **Days in March**

 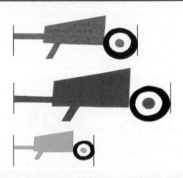

Draw more Xs to show the number. Write the number.
Count the pennies. Write how many cents.
Look at the calendar. Write how many days in March.
Circle the group of objects that are in order from shortest to longest, starting at the top.

Circle the container that holds more. Mark an X on the container that holds less.

🐟 🐢 ⭐ ❤️ Circle the container that holds more. Mark an X on the container that holds less.

🏠 HOME ACTIVITY • Set out several small food items, such as marshmallows, or larger ones, such as apples. Ask your child to find a container that is just the right size to hold them.

Name _____

Compare Weight

 **Left**

Right

Hold one object in your left hand and one object in your right hand. Circle the picture of the object that feels heavier.

Left **Right**

🐟 🐋 ⭐ **Hold one object in your left hand and one object in your right hand. Mark an X on the picture of the object that feels lighter.**

⬠ **HOME ACTIVITY** • Give your child two objects of clearly different weights. Have him or her hold one in each hand and tell which feels heavier.

© Harcourt

234

PROBLEM SOLVING

What is wrong in this picture? Circle the things
that are unlikely to happen when the weather is hot.
What is wrong in this picture? Circle the things
that are unlikely to happen when the weather is cold.

© Harcourt

🐟🐋⭐❤️🌸🦋 Use red to circle the pictures that most likely show hot weather. Use blue to circle the pictures that most likely show cold weather.

🏠 HOME ACTIVITY • Have your child describe what he or she would wear when the weather is hot and when it is cold.

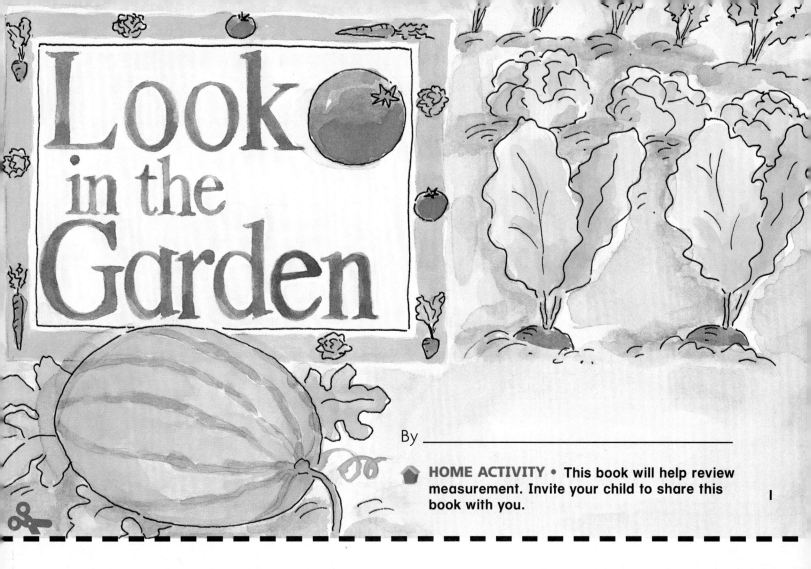

Look in the Garden

By _____

🔷 HOME ACTIVITY • This book will help review measurement. Invite your child to share this book with you.

1

Circle the shorter worm.

3

Circle the longer caterpillar.

Circle the longest cricket.

Circle the shortest lizard.

✂ -- -- -- -- -- -- -- -- -- -- -- -- -- -- -- -- --

Circle the lighter object.

Circle the heavier object.

6

**Circle the basket that
holds more.**

8

Circle the bucket that holds less.

Is it hot or cold? How do you know?

Is it hot or cold?
How do you know?

Look in the garden.
What do you see?

Name _____

✔️ Review

🐟 🐢 **Circle the container that holds more. Mark an X on the container that holds less.**

⭐ **Hold one object in your left hand and one object in your right hand. Mark an X on the object that feels heavier.**

♥ **Use red to circle the picture that most likely shows hot weather. Use blue to circle the picture that most likely shows cold weather.**

✔ Cumulative Review

 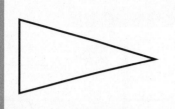 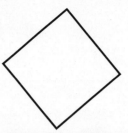 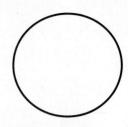

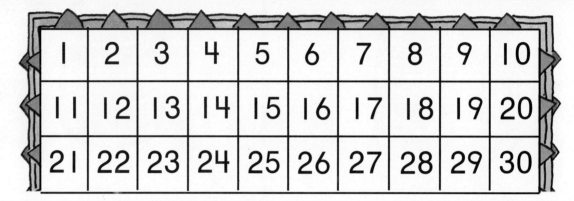

1	2	3	4	5	6	7	8	9	10
11	12	13	14	15	16	17	18	19	20
21	22	23	24	25	26	27	28	29	30

🐟 Look at the object at the beginning of the row. Color in the outline that matches the shape of the object.

🐢 Use yellow to color the numbers you say when you count by fives. Use blue to circle the numbers you say when you count by tens. What patterns do you see?

⭐ Go on a measurement walk. Use yarn of different colors to measure the desk and the shelves. Cut the yarn and compare the two pieces. Circle the picture of the place where you used the longer piece.

♥ Circle the container that holds more. Mark an X on the container that holds less.

Name _____

✅ Test

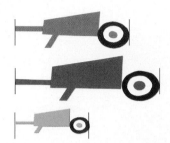

_____

- - - - - -

_____ **cubes**

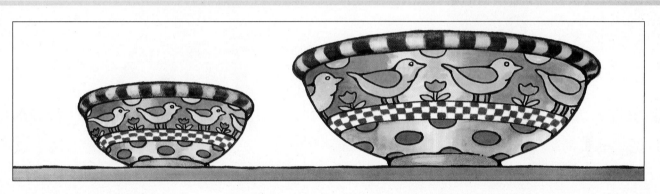

 Circle the group of objects that are in order from shortest to longest, starting at the top.
 Use cubes to measure the vegetable. About how many cubes long is it? Write the number.
 Circle the container that holds more. Mark an X on the container that holds less.
 Hold one object in your left hand and one object in your right hand. Mark an X on the object that feels lighter.

© Harcourt

239

CHALLENGE
How Far?

short steps

LONG STEPS

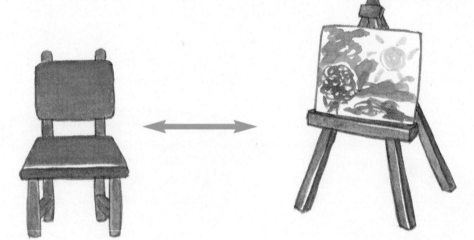

short steps

LONG STEPS

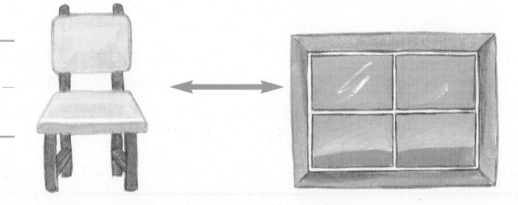

short steps

LONG STEPS

Use short steps to measure how far it is from your chair to each place. Write the number of short steps you walked.
Use LONG STEPS to measure how far it is from your chair to each place. Write the number of LONG STEPS you walked.

240

Data, Graphing, and Probability

Sort the shapes. Draw your groups in the sorting rings.

For permission to reprint copyrighted material, grateful acknowledgment is made to the following sources:

Barefoot Books Ltd.: Cover illustration by Debbie Harter from *Bear in a Square* by Stella Blackstone. Illustration copyright © 1998 by Debbie Harter.

Margaret K. McElderry Books, Simon & Schuster Children's Publishing Division: Cover illustration by Keiko Narahashi from *What's what?* by Mary Serfozo. Illustration copyright © 1996 by Keiko Narahashi.

Random House Children's Books, a division of Random House, Inc.: Cover illustration by Jose Aruego and Ariane Dewey from *Five Little Ducks* by Raffi. Illustration copyright © 1989 by Jose Aruego and Ariane Dewey.
Printed in the United States of America

Photography Credits:

All photography by Harcourt photographers listed, © Harcourt: Weronica Ankarorn, Victoria Bowen, Ken Kinzie, Sheri O'Neal, Quebecor Imaging, and Terry Sinclair.

Illustration Credits:

Joe Boddy: 245, 246, 251, 252, 255, 256, 259, 260, 263, 264; **Sharon Holm:** 247, 248, 249, 250; **Richard Kolding:** 261, 262; **Kurt Nagahori:** 244; **Ken Spengler:** storybook; **Matt Straub:** 242, 243; **Stan Tusan:** 257, 258; **Mary O'Keefe Young:** cover.

© Harcourt

SCHOOL HOME CONNECTION

☀ Dear Family,

Today we started a new chapter, Data, Graphing, and Probability. In this chapter we will learn more about graphs and about tally tables. We will also learn when something is more likely or less likely to happen.

Love,

_____

Vocabulary Power

1   **2**   **3**   **4**   **5**

tally marks

Lunch

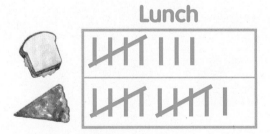

tally table

Visit *The Learning Site* for additional ideas and activities.
www.harcourtschool.com

ACTIVITY

- Give your child several buttons, some with two holes and some with four holes. Have him or her sort the buttons. Then ask your child to make a tally table showing how he or she sorted.

BOOKS TO SHARE

To read more about data and graphing with your child, look for these books in your local library.

What's what?
by Mary Serfozo.
Simon & Schuster, 1996.

Is It Rough? Is It Smooth? Is It Shiny?
by Tana Hoban. Greenwillow, 1984.

Who Hops?
by Katie Davis. Harcourt, 1998.

243

MATERIALS: crayons, paper clip, pencils
DIRECTIONS: Play with a partner and decide who goes first. The first player spins the spinner and draws that shape in the correct column of his or her graph. Take turns. The first player to fill a column wins.

244

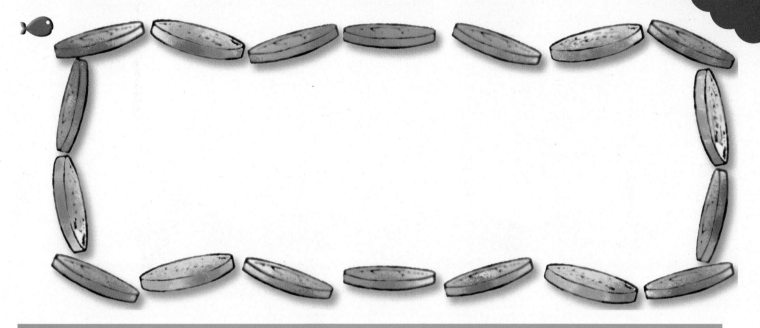

 ## How Many Pennies and Nickels?

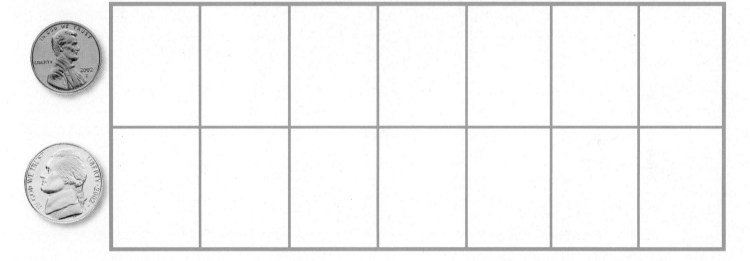

 _____

_____

penny

 _____

_____

nickel

 Place a handful of coins on the workspace. Sort your coins.

Make a graph with your coins.

Write how many of each coin. Circle the number that shows more coins. Mark an X on the number that shows fewer coins.

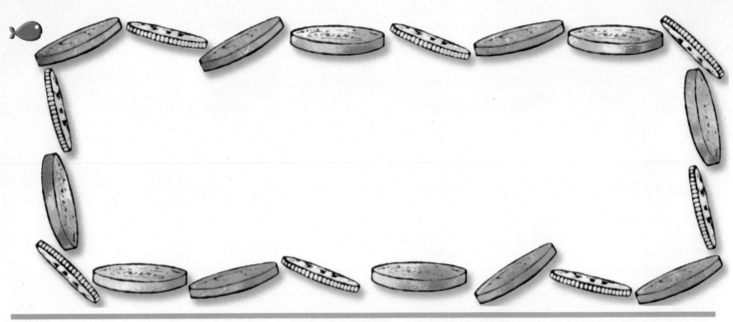

 ## How Many Coins?

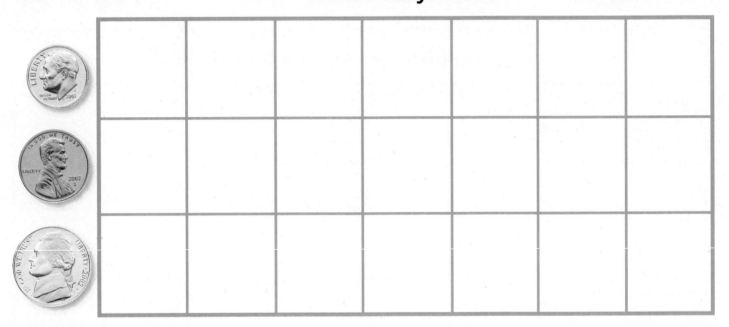

dime   **penny**   **nickel**

Place a handful of coins on the workspace. Sort your coins.

Make a graph with your coins.

Write how many of each coin. Circle the number that shows the most coins. Mark an X on the number that shows the fewest coins.

HOME ACTIVITY • Have your child explain to you how he or she made the coin graph on this page.

© Harcourt

Where We Played

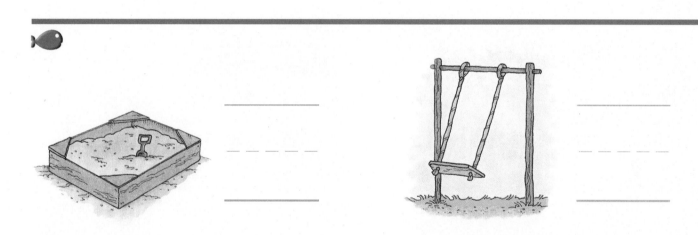

🐟 **Use the graph. Write how many in each group.**
🐢 **Circle the place where more children played.**

Books We Read

_____

_____

_____

 Use the graph. Write how many in each group.
 Circle the book that fewer children read.

HOME ACTIVITY • Ask your child to explain how the graph on this page shows which book more children read.

Make Picture Graphs

Shirts

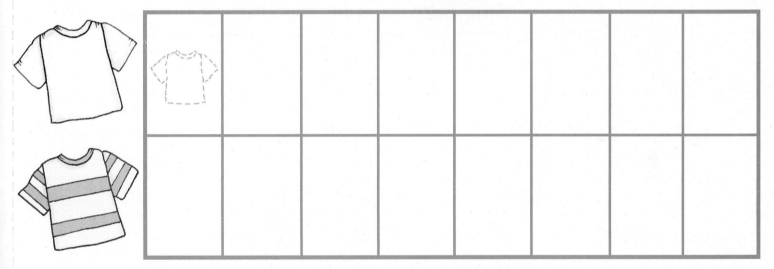

 _ _ _ _ _ _ _ _ _ _ _

 _ _ _ _ _ _ _ _ _ _ _

 Look at the picture. Make a picture graph about plain shirts and striped shirts.

Write how many of each kind of shirt. Circle the number that shows more.

 Girls and Boys in the Library

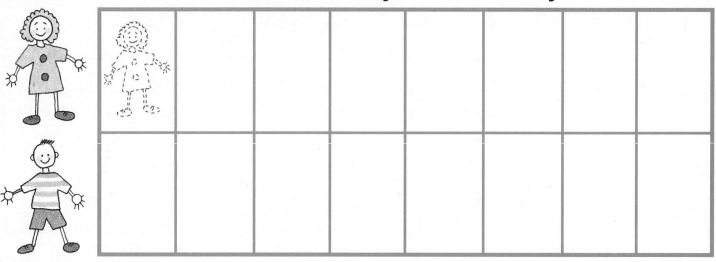

 Look at the picture. Make a graph about girls and boys.

Write how many girls and how many boys. Circle the number that shows fewer.

HOME ACTIVITY • Have your child explain the graph he or she made on this page.

Name _____

Party Balloons

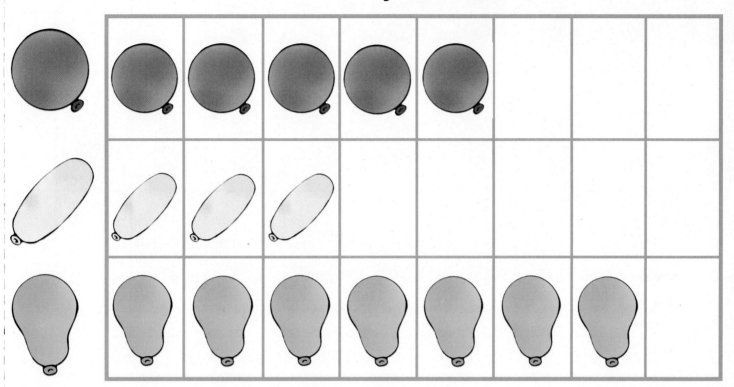

_____   _____   _____

_____   _____   _____

_____   _____   _____

Look at the graph. Write how many of each kind of balloon. Circle the number that shows the most balloons. Mark an X on the number that shows the fewest balloons.

Party Gifts

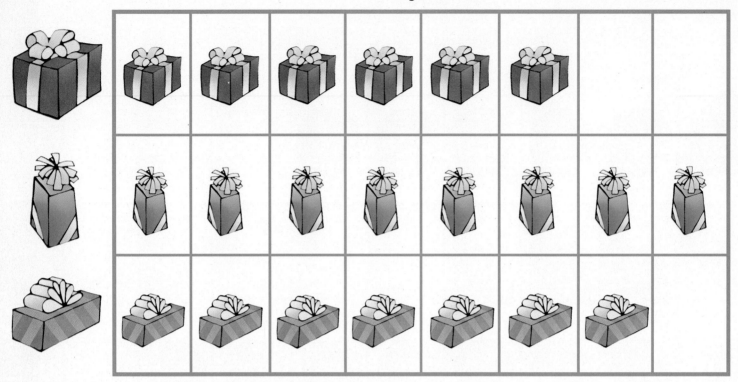

_____ _____ _____

_ _ _ _ _ _ _ _ _ _ _ _ _ _ _

_____ _____ _____

Look at the graph. Write how many of each kind of gift. Which number shows the kind there were the most of at the party? How do you know? Circle the number.

© Harcourt

HOME ACTIVITY • Have your child ask family members about their favorite color and then make a graph to show the information he or she gathered.

Name _____

 **Review**

Shapes

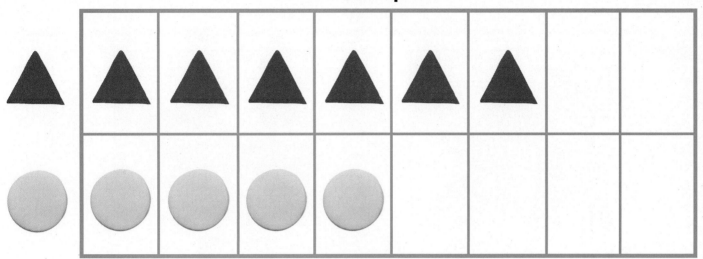

 Use the graph. Write how many in each group.
 Circle the picture that shows which group has more shapes.

 **Cumulative Review**

10

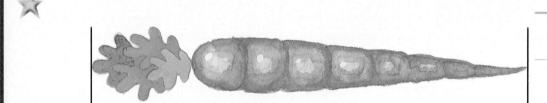

_____ **cubes**

Build the cube train. Take one cube from each end of the train and snap these cubes together. Do this as many times as you can. If you have only pairs, the number is even. Circle the number. If you have one cube left over, the number is odd. Mark an X on the number.

What times of day do the pictures show? Circle the time of day that is missing.

Use cubes to measure the carrot. Write the number that tells about how many cubes long.

Hold one object in your left hand and one object in your right hand. Mark an X on the object that feels lighter.

© Harcourt

254

Name _____

Ways We Go To School

   _____      _____

🐟 Look at the table. Write how many for each way.
🐢 Circle the picture that shows the way more
children go to school.

Sports We Played

	Ⅼ Ⅼ Ⅼ Ⅼ
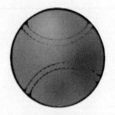	Ⅼ Ⅼ Ⅼ
	Ⅼ Ⅼ Ⅼ Ⅼ Ⅼ Ⅼ Ⅼ

         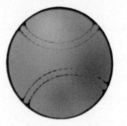   

_____   _____   _____

- - - - - - - -   - - - - - - - -   - - - - - - - -

_____   _____   _____

 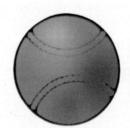     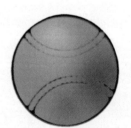 

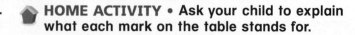

Look at the table. Write how many for each sport.
Circle the ball that shows which sport the most children played.
Circle the ball that shows which sport the fewest children played.

HOME ACTIVITY • Ask your child to explain what each mark on the table stands for.

256

Name _____

Do You Have a Pet?

Yes

No

Yes _____   No _____

_____

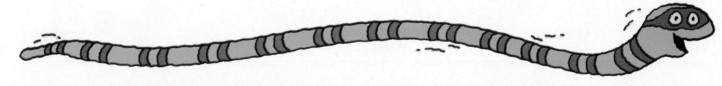

Ask five classmates if they have a pet. Make a tally table.

Write how many for each answer. Circle the number that is greater. Do more of the children you asked have a pet or not have a pet? How do you know?

257

Are You Wearing Yellow?

Yes	
No	

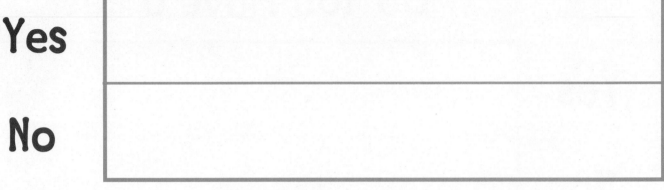

Yes _____   No _____

_____

Ask five classmates if they are wearing yellow. Make a tally table.

Write how many for each answer. Circle the number that is less. Are fewer of the children you asked wearing yellow or not wearing yellow? How do you know?

HOME ACTIVITY • Have your child ask family members if they like pizza. Help him or her make a tally table to show the results.

Name _____

Red and Blue

Use a paper clip and a pencil to make a spinner. Spin ten times.
Make a tally mark in the table after each spin. Which color did the
paper clip land on more often? Why did this happen? Circle the
row with more tally marks.

259

Blue and Red

Use a paper clip and a pencil to make a spinner. Spin ten times. Make a tally mark in the table after each spin. Which color did the paper clip land on more often? Why did this happen? Circle the row with more tally marks.

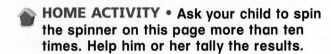

HOME ACTIVITY • Ask your child to spin the spinner on this page more than ten times. Help him or her tally the results.

260

Circle the picture that shows which is more likely to happen.

 Circle the picture that shows which is less likely to happen.

 HOME ACTIVITY • Use phrases such as "Could that really happen?" or "Is that likely to happen?" with your child to help him or her explore probability.

Name ______________________________

Problem Solving Skill
Make a Prediction

Ask two classmates how many pockets they have.
Draw a picture to show how many pockets in all.
Write how many pockets the two classmates have.
Do you think four classmates will have more or fewer pockets?

Ask four classmates how many pockets they have. Draw a picture to show how many pockets in all. Write how many pockets the four classmates have. What did you learn?

 HOME ACTIVITY • Have your child explain to you how he or she predicted whether four children would have more or fewer pockets than two children.

What's for Lunch?

By _____

⬠ **HOME ACTIVITY** • This book will help review graphs. Invite your child to share this book with you.

1

We want tacos!

3

We want sandwiches!

5

We want pizza!

7

How many want pizza?

6

Time for lunch!

8

© Harcourt

✔ Review

Ways We Go To School

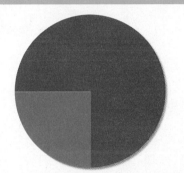

Red and Blue

🐟 Look at the tally table. Write how many. Circle the picture that shows how more children go to school.

🐢 Use a paper clip and a pencil to make a spinner. Spin ten times. Make a tally mark in the table after each spin. Circle the row with more tally marks.

⭐ Circle the picture that shows which is more likely to happen.

♥ Circle the picture that shows which is less likely to happen.

✔ Cumulative Review

 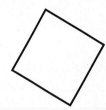 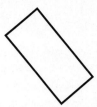 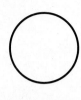

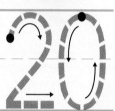

Where We Played

    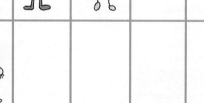

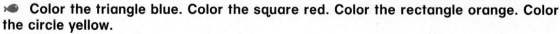

🐟 Color the triangle blue. Color the square red. Color the rectangle orange. Color the circle yellow.

🐢 Count by fives. Trace the number.

⭐ Circle the container that holds more. Mark an X on the container that holds less.

♥ Use the graph. Write how many in each group. Circle the number that shows where more children played.

266

Name _____

✔ Test

Books We Read

_____

_ _ _ _ _ _ _ _

_____

_____

_ _ _ _ _ _ _ _

Red and Blue

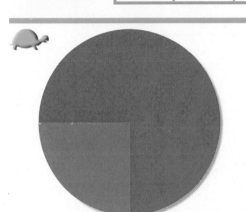 

🐟 **Use the graph. Write how many in each group. Circle the number that shows which book fewer children read.**

🐢 **Use a paper clip and a pencil to make a spinner. Spin ten times. Make a tally mark in the table after each spin. Circle the row with more tally marks.**

⭐ **Circle the picture that shows which is more likely to happen.**

♥ **Circle the picture that shows which is less likely to happen.**

CHALLENGE
Penny Graphs

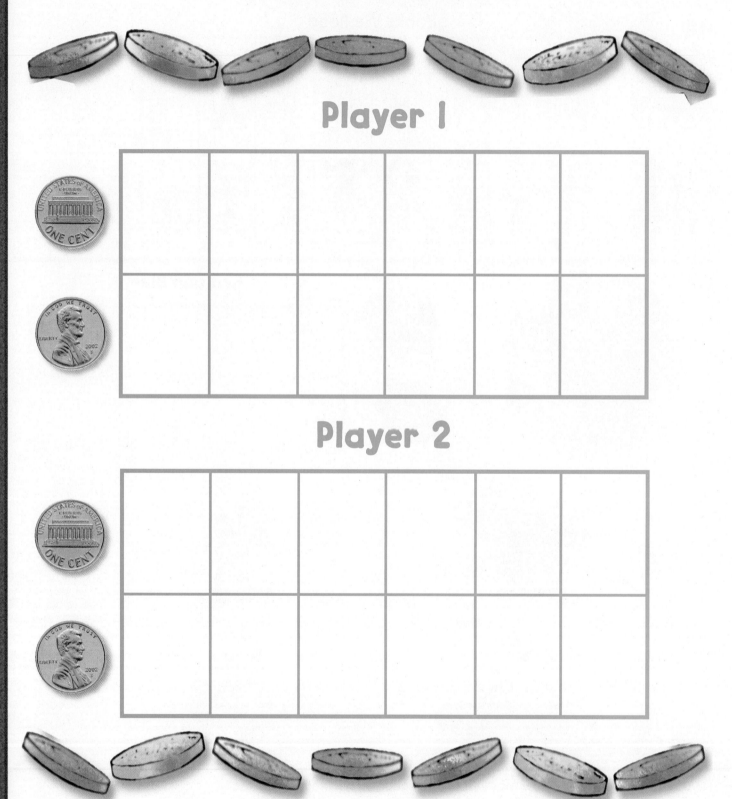

Player 1

Player 2

Play with a partner. Flip a penny. Color a square in the graph to show if it landed on heads or tails. When one player has filled a row, compare graphs.

CHAPTER

11

Addition

HARCOURT

Math

Harcourt

Circle the group that has more pennies.

Photography Credits:

All photography by Harcourt photographers listed, © Harcourt: Weronica Ankarorn, Victoria Bowen, Ken Kinzie, Sheri O'Neal, Quebecor Imaging, and Terry Sinclair.

Illustration Credits:

Liz Allen: 285, 286; **Tuko Fujisaki:** 271; **Obadinah Heavner:** Storybook; **Betsey James:** 273, 274; **Chris Lensch:** 283, 284; **Claude Martinot:** 277, 278; **Dan McGeehan:** 279, 280; **Jill Meyerhoff:** 275, 276, 289, 290; **Pamela Thompson:** cover; **Greg Valley:** 272; **Kathy Wilburn:** 287, 288; **James Williamson:** 270.

© Harcourt

SCHOOL HOME CONNECTION

Dear Family,

Today we started a new chapter, Addition. We will learn to join two groups to find out how many in all. We will also read and complete addition sentences.

Love,

_____

Vocabulary Power

in all

5 bugs and 3 bugs is 8 bugs in all

addition sentence

$5 + 3 = 8$

5 plus 3 equals 8

ACTIVITY

- Play a shopping game. Tag some small objects with prices from 1¢ to 5¢. Have your child use pennies to "buy" two objects.

BOOKS TO SHARE

To read about addition with your child, look for these books in your local library.

The Crayon Counting Book, by Pam Muñoz Ryan and Jerry Pallotta. Charlesbridge Publishing, 1996.

What! Cried Granny, by Kate Lum. Penguin Putnam, 1999.

Visit *The Learning Site* for additional ideas and activities. www.harcourtschool.com

Math Game

MATERIALS: game marker for each player, number cube (1–6)
DIRECTIONS: Players take turns tossing the number cube and moving that many spaces. Each player adds 1 to the number on which he or she lands. If the player adds correctly, the marker stays on that space. If not, the marker goes back to where it was. The first player to reach END wins.

272

3

© Harcourt

Listen to and act out the story. One
more child is joining the group. Write the
number that tells how many children in all.

Listen to and act out the story. More children come to play. Write the number that tells how many children in all.

HOME ACTIVITY • Make two stacks of books. Ask your child to count the books in each stack and then find how many books in all.

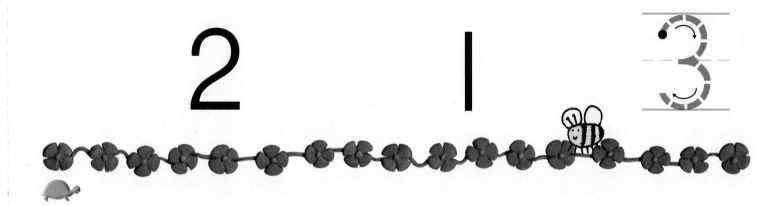

2   1   3

7   3

5   4

Listen to the story. Model the story with connecting cubes.
Write the number that tells how many in all.

© Harcourt

275

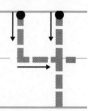

2   2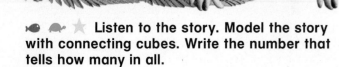

4   3 _____

6   2 _____

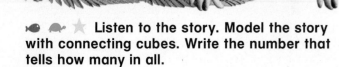 **Listen to the story. Model the story with connecting cubes. Write the number that tells how many in all.**

⬠ **HOME ACTIVITY** • Tell your child a very short story about adding 1 object to a group of 4 objects. Have your child model the story with small objects and write the number that tells how many objects in all.

276

1 + 1 =

2 + 1 =

3 + 1 =

4 + 1 =

Count the birds on the branch. Then draw one more bird coming. Write the number that tells how many birds in all.

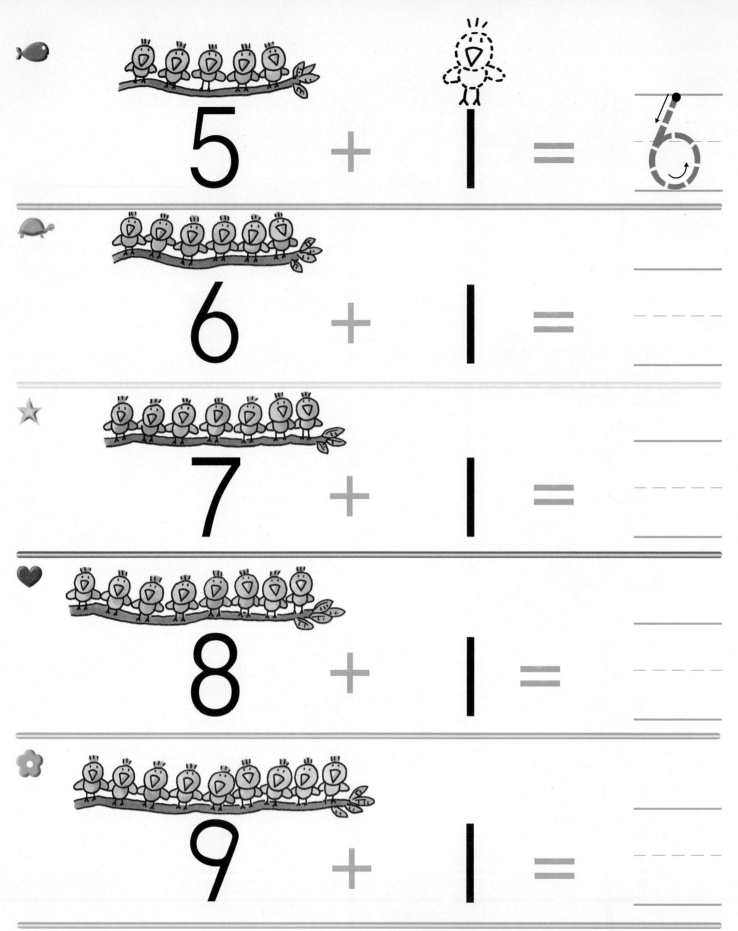

5 + 1 = 6

6 + 1 =

7 + 1 =

8 + 1 =

9 + 1 =

Count the birds on the branch. Then draw one more bird coming. Write the number that tells how many birds in all.

HOME ACTIVITY • Tell your child an addition story that adds one more. Encourage your child to use objects or drawings to act out the story.

Name _____

Use Pictures to Add

 + 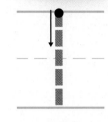 =

___ + ___ = ___

⭐

___ + ___ = ___

 Tell a story about the pictures. Complete the addition sentence.

© Harcourt

279

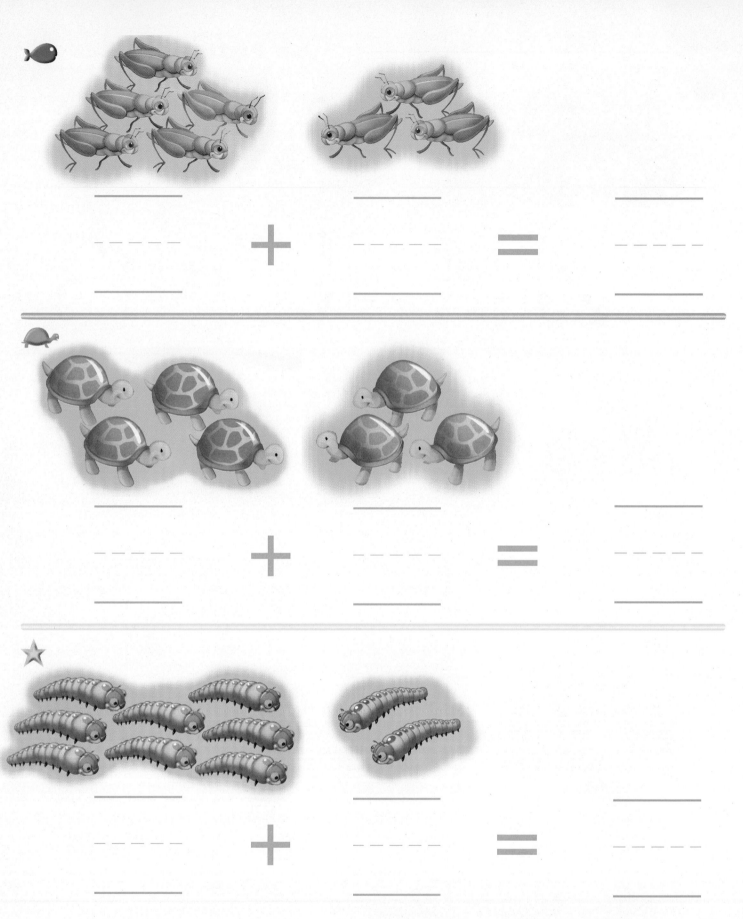

_____ + _____ = _____

_____ + _____ = _____

_____ + _____ = _____

🐟 🐢 ⭐ Tell a story about the pictures.
Complete the addition sentence.

⬠ **HOME ACTIVITY** • Ask your child to draw a
picture that shows the adding of two groups.

280

Name _____

 Review

| 4 | 3 | _____ |

6 **+** 1 **=** _____

_____ **+** _____ **=** _____

_____ **+** _____ **=** _____

 Listen to the story. Model the story with connecting cubes. Write the number that tells how many in all.

 Count the birds on the branch. Then draw one more bird coming. Write the number that tells how many birds in all.

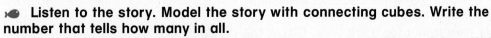 Tell a story about the pictures. Complete the addition sentence.

281

✅ Cumulative Review

_____   **+**   _____   **=**   _____

Ways We Go To School

| | | |
✦✦✦✦✦

_____
_____
_____

🐟 Tell a story about the pictures. Complete the addition sentence.
🐢 Circle the longer object. Underline the shorter object.
★ Look at the tally table. Write how many for each way. Circle the picture that shows how more children go to school.
❤ Circle the picture that shows which is more likely to happen.

282

Name _____

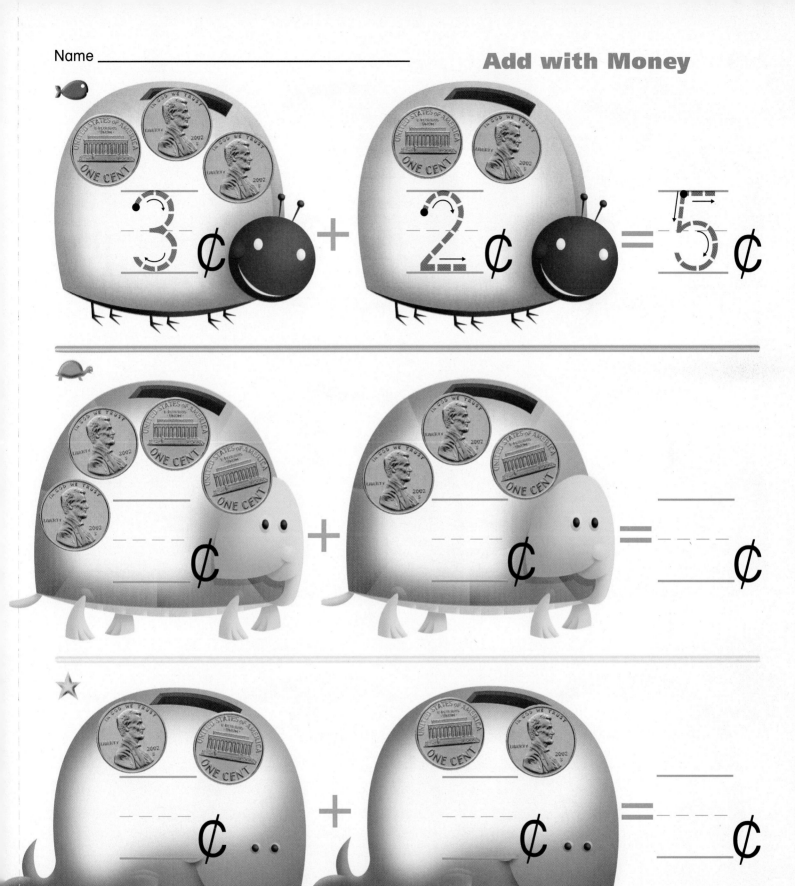

3 ¢ + 2 ¢ = 5 ¢

_____ ¢ + _____ ¢ = _____ ¢

_____ ¢ + _____ ¢ = _____ ¢

🐟 🐠 ⭐ Count the pennies in each bank. Write
how many cents. Add. Write how many cents in all.

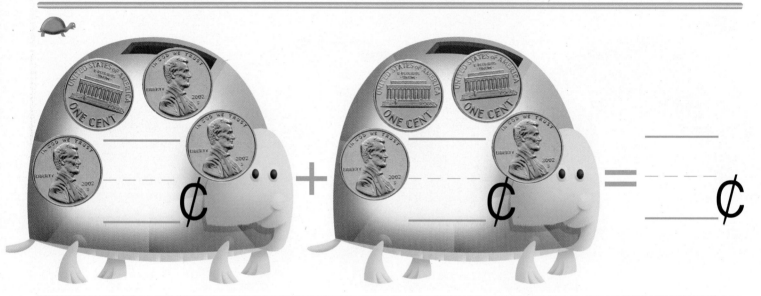

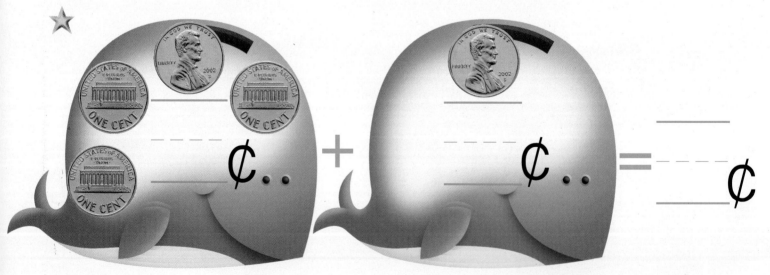

Count the pennies in each bank. Write how many cents. Add. Write how many cents in all.

HOME ACTIVITY • Have your child use real pennies to model these addition problems.

284

 +  =

____ + ____ = ____

____ + ____ = ____

🐟 🐢 ⭐ **Tell a story about the animals.**
Complete the addition sentence.

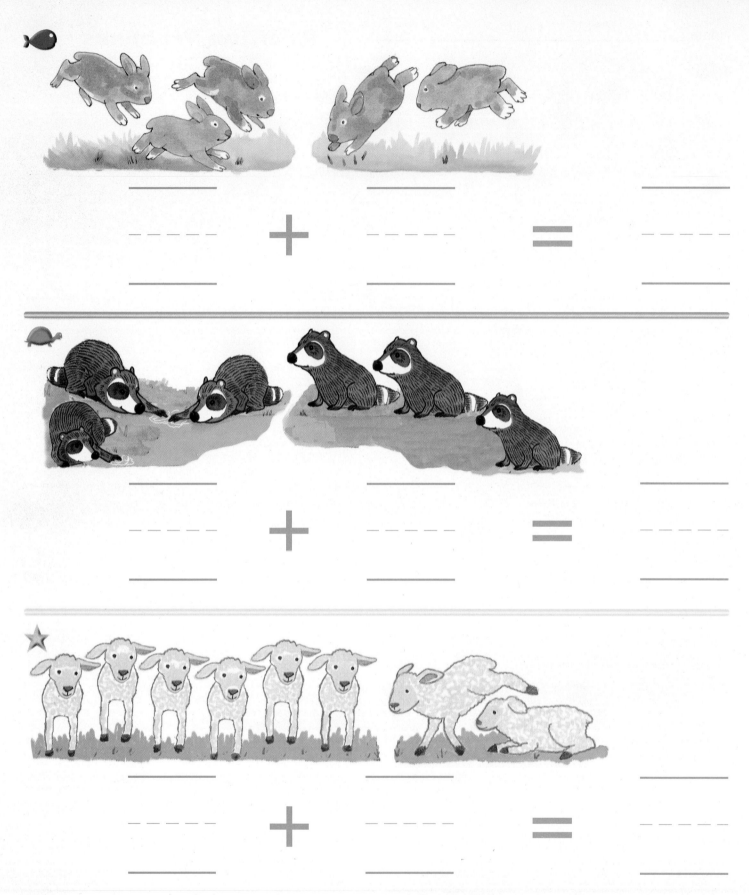

Tell a story about the animals in the picture. Write the addition sentence.

HOME ACTIVITY • Have your child draw simple animals to show adding groups. Then help him or her write the addition sentence.

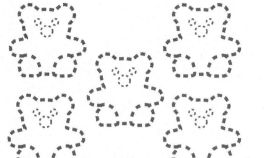

 +  =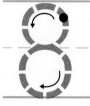

_____ + _____ = _____

  **Tell an addition story. Act out your story with objects.
Draw the objects. Then complete the addition sentence.**

287

$$\underline{\qquad} + \underline{\qquad} = \underline{\qquad}$$

$$\underline{\qquad} + \underline{\qquad} = \underline{\qquad}$$

Tell an addition story. Act out your story with objects. Draw the objects. Then complete the addition sentence.

HOME ACTIVITY • Have your child create and act out an addition story using objects.

© Harcourt

4 + 1 = **5**

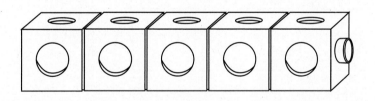

____ + ____ = **5**

Use blue and yellow connecting cubes to show different ways to make 5. Color the cubes. Write the numbers for each color to complete the addition sentence.

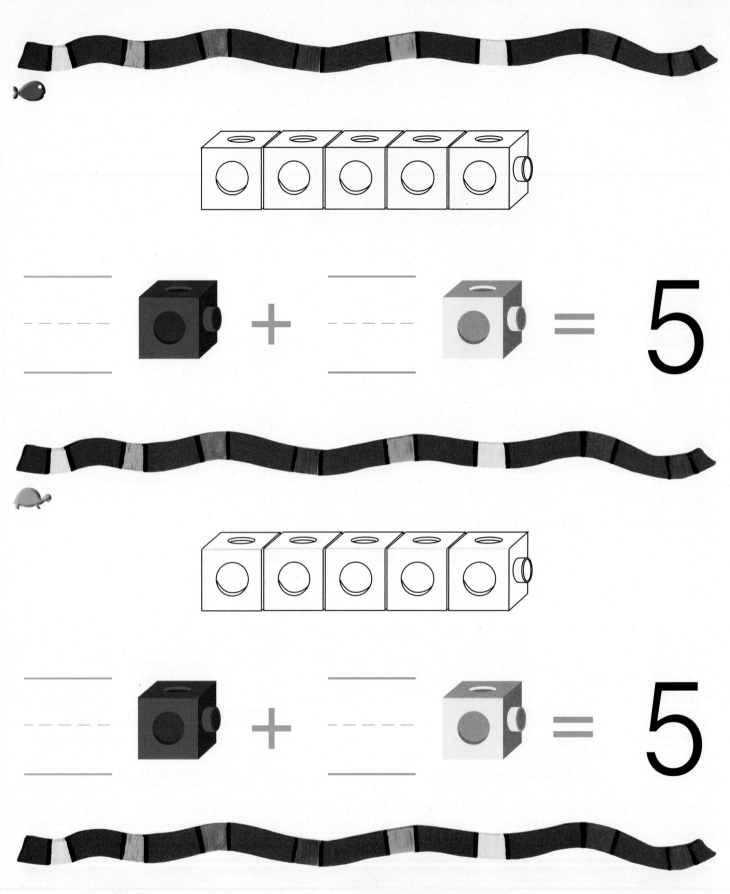

_____ + _____ = 5

_____ + _____ = 5

🐟🐢 Use blue and yellow connecting cubes to show different ways to make 5. Color the cubes. Write the numbers for each color to complete the addition sentence.

⬠ **HOME ACTIVITY** • Write three addition problems that each add up to 5. Give your child 5 pennies to use to model the problems, using heads for the first number and tails for the second number.

Our Home

By _____

⬡ **HOME ACTIVITY** • This book will help review
addition. Invite your child to share this book
with you.

1

$$2 + 1 = \underline{\quad}$$

3

2 bees

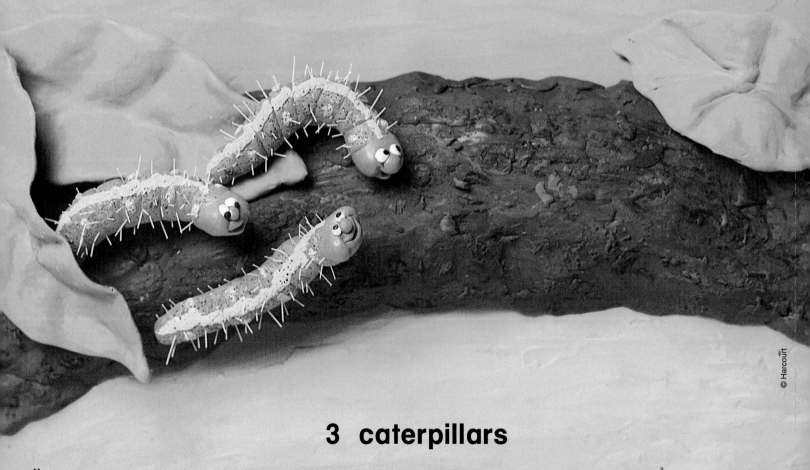

3 caterpillars

$$3 + 2 = \underline{\hspace{2cm}}$$

$$4 + 4 = \underline{\hspace{2cm}}$$

4 baby birds

5 squirrels

5 + 4 = ____

8 + 2 = ____

8 birds

Welcome to our home!

Name _____

✔️ Review

_ _ _ _ _   +   _ _ _ _ _   =   _ _ _ _ _

_ _ _ _ _   +   _ _ _ _ _   =   _ _ _ _ _

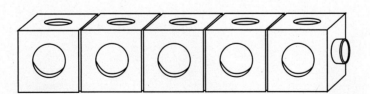

 _ _ _ _ _    +   _ _ _ _ _   =    5

🐟 Tell a story about the ducks in the picture. Complete the addition sentence.

🐢 Tell an addition story. Act out your story with objects. Draw the objects and complete the addition sentence.

⭐ Use blue and yellow connecting cubes to show different ways to make five. Color the cubes. Write the numbers that tell how many of each color.

© Harcourt

291

✅ Cumulative Review

🐟 4 5 6 ■ 8

2
7

🐢

1	2	3	4	5	6	7	8	9	10
11	12	13	14	15	16	17	18	19	20
21	22	23	24	25	26	27	28	29	30

⭐

❤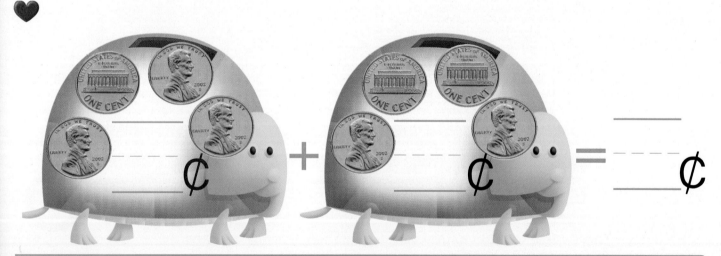

___ ¢ + ___ ¢ = ___ ¢

🐟 Circle the missing number.
🐋 Color to finish the pattern. Touch and count by twos.
⭐ Use red to circle the picture that most likely shows hot weather.
Use blue to circle the picture that mostly likely shows cold weather.
❤ Count the pennies in each bank. Write how many. Add. Write how many in all.

Name _____

 Test

5 + 1 = _____

_____ + _____ = _____

_____ + _____ = _____

 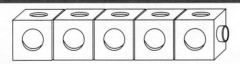

_____  + _____ = 5

 Count the birds on the branch. Then draw one more bird coming. Write the number that tells how many birds in all.

 Tell a story about the frogs in the picture. Complete the addition sentence.

 Tell an addition story. Act out your story with objects. Draw the objects and complete the addition sentence.

 Use blue and yellow connecting cubes to show different ways to make five. Color the cubes. Write the numbers that tell how many of each color.

CHALLENGE

Dimes and Pennies

10¢ + _____ ¢ = _____ ¢

_____ ¢ + _____ ¢ = 12¢

_____ ¢ + 3¢ = _____ ¢

10¢ + _____ ¢ = _____ ¢

   Complete the addition sentence.

294

CHAPTER 12

Subtraction

🐟 🐢 ⭐ **Count the turtles. Draw a group that has one fewer.**

Photography Credits:

All photography by Harcourt photographers listed, © Harcourt: Weronica Ankarorn, Victoria Bowen, Ken Kinzie, Sheri O'Neal, Quebecor Imaging, and Terry Sinclair.

Illustration Credits:

Ken Bowser: 305, 306, 309, 310, 311, 312; **Priscilla Burris:** storybook; **Susan Calitri:** 315, 316; **Daniel Del Valle:** 242; **Kathy Ember:** cover; **Tim Haggerty:** 298; **Obadinah Heavner:** 313, 314; **Betsey James:** 299, 300; **Heidi King:** 242; **Dan McGeehan:** 242; **Stan Tusan:** 297; **Sally Vitsky:** 301, 302.

© Harcourt

SCHOOL HOME CONNECTION

☀ Dear Family,

Today we started a new chapter, Subtraction. We will learn to subtract objects from a larger group of objects. We will also learn to read and complete subtraction sentences.

Love,

_____

Vocabulary Power

take away, are left

There are 3 birds.
1 bird flies away.
Now 2 birds are left.

subtraction sentence

$$3 - 1 = 2$$

3 minus 1 equals 2.

ACTIVITY

- Have your child use objects and make up a story in which some of the objects are taken away.

BOOKS TO SHARE

To read about subtraction with your child, look for these books at your local library.

Ten Little Mice, by Joyce Dunbar. Gulliver, 1990.

Elevator Magic, by Stuart J. Murphy. HarperCollins, 1997.

10, 9, 8, by Molly Bang. HarperCollins, 2000.

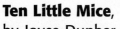

 Visit *The Learning Site* for additional ideas and activities. www.harcourtschool.com

Math Game

START

END

MATERIALS: game marker for each player, number cube (1–6)
DIRECTIONS: Players take turns tossing the number cube and moving that many spaces. Each player subtracts 1 from the number on which he or she lands. If the player subtracts correctly, the marker stays on that space. If not, the marker goes back to where it was. The first player to reach END wins.

298

© Harcourt

Problem Solving Strategy
Act It Out

_____
- - - - -
_____

_____
- - - - -
_____

Listen to and act out the story. Count how many are left. Write the number that tells how many are left.

© Harcourt

🐟 🐢 Listen to and act out the story. Count how many are left. Write the number that tells how many are left.

🏠 **HOME ACTIVITY** • Make a stack of 5 books. Have your child count the books. Take 2 books away, and have your child count the books that are left.

© Harcourt

300

Model Subtraction

5   3   2

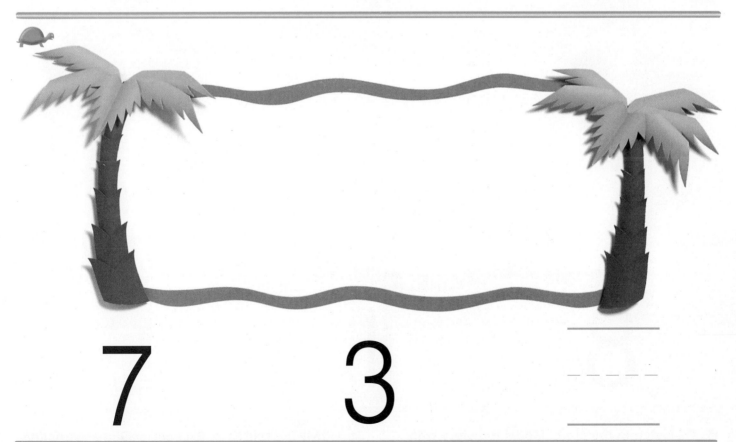

7   3

Listen to the story. Model the story with connecting cubes. Write the number that tells how many are left.

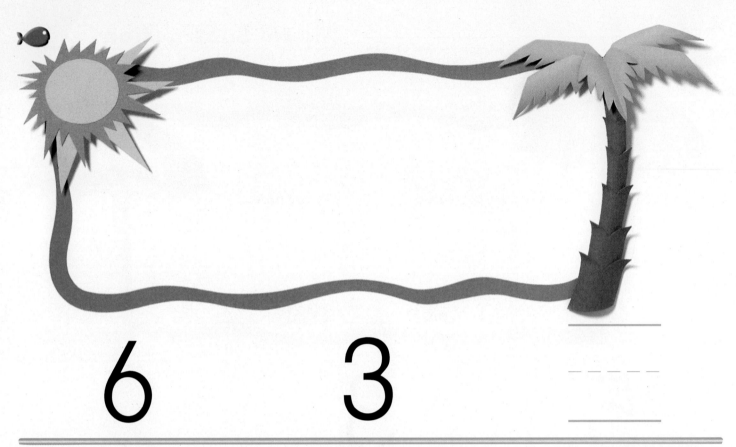

6   3   _____

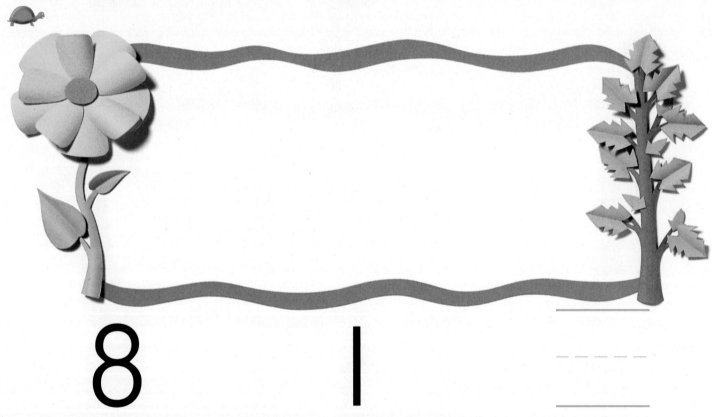

8   1   _____

Listen to the story. Model the story with connecting cubes. Write the number that tells how many are left.

HOME ACTIVITY • Tell your child a subtraction story about having 4 crackers and eating 2 of them. Have your child act out the story, using real crackers, and tell you how many crackers are left.

10 − 1 = 9

9 − 1 =

8 − 1 =

7 − 1 =

🐟 🐢 ⭐ ❤ Count the pelicans. Mark an X on the pelican that is
flying away. Write the number that tells how many pelicans are left.

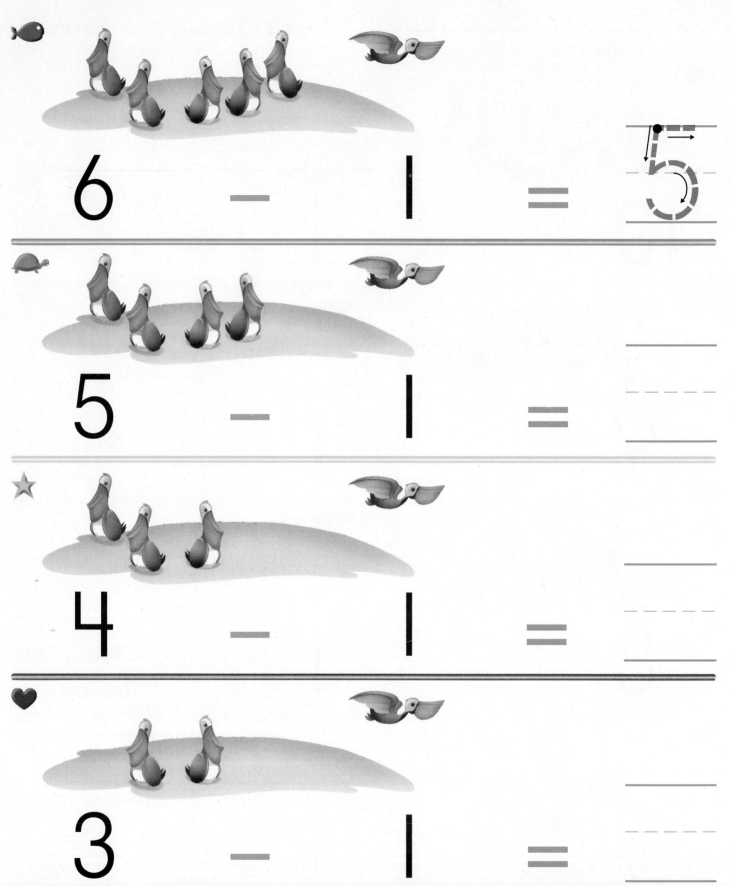

6 − 1 = 5

5 − 1 = ___

4 − 1 = ___

3 − 1 = ___

Count the pelicans. Mark an X on the pelican that is flying away. Write the number that tells how many pelicans are left.

HOME ACTIVITY • Have your child tell you about the number pattern on this page.

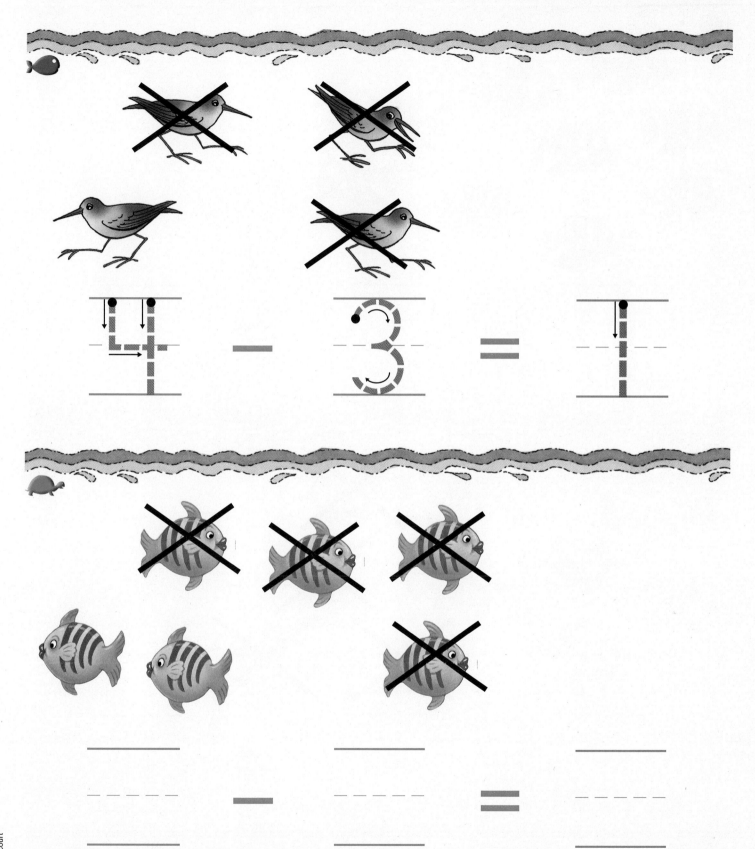

🐟 🐢 **Tell the subtraction story. Complete the subtraction sentence.**

305

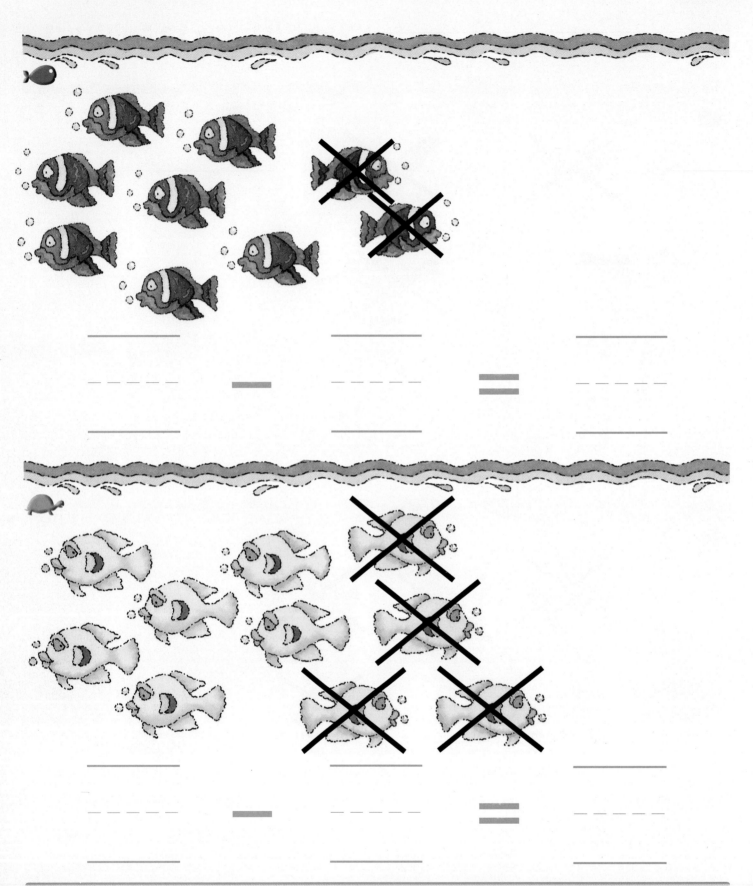

_____ _____ _____ _____ _____

_____ _____ _____ _____ _____

🐟 🐢 Tell the subtraction story. Complete the subtraction sentence.

🏠 **HOME ACTIVITY** • Encourage your child to tell a subtraction story. You may wish to have your child draw the subtraction story.

© Harcourt

306

Name _____

✔️ Review

7   3

_____

_____

10   —   1   =   _ _ _ _ _

_____   —   _____   =   _____

_ _ _ _ _   _ _ _ _ _   _ _ _ _ _

_____   —   _____   =   _____

_ _ _ _ _   _ _ _ _ _   _ _ _ _ _

© Harcourt

🐟 **Listen to the story. Model the story with connecting cubes. Write the number that tells how many are left.**

🐢 **Count the pelicans. Mark an X on the pelican that is flying away. Write the number that tells how many pelicans are left.**

⭐ ❤️ **Tell the subtraction story. Complete the subtraction sentence.**

0 ___ 2 3 ___ 5

March

Sunday	Monday	Tuesday	Wednesday	Thursday	Friday	Saturday
	1	2	3	4	5	6
7	8	9	10	11	12	13
14	15	16	17	18	19	20
21	22	23	24	25	26	27
28	29	30	31			

_____ **Saturdays**

_____ **Days in March**

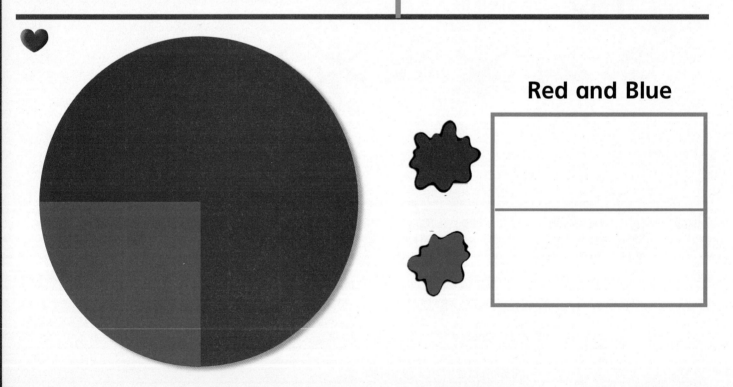

Red and Blue

🐟 Write the number that is before two. Write the number that is after three.
🐢 Look at the calendar. Count the Saturdays. Write how many.
⭐ Look at the calendar. Write how many days in March.
❤ Use a paper clip and a pencil to make a spinner. Spin ten times. Make a tally mark in the table after each spin. Circle the row with more tally marks.

Name _____

Subtract with Money

5 ¢   —   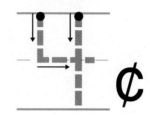 4 ¢   =    1 ¢

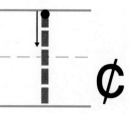

_____ ¢   —   _____ ¢   =   _____ ¢

Listen to the story. Complete the subtraction
sentence to tell how much money is left.

_____ ¢   —   _____ ¢   =   _____ ¢

_____ ¢   —   _____ ¢   =   _____ ¢

Listen to the story. Complete the subtraction sentence to tell how much money is left.

HOME ACTIVITY • Have your child use real pennies to model these subtraction problems.

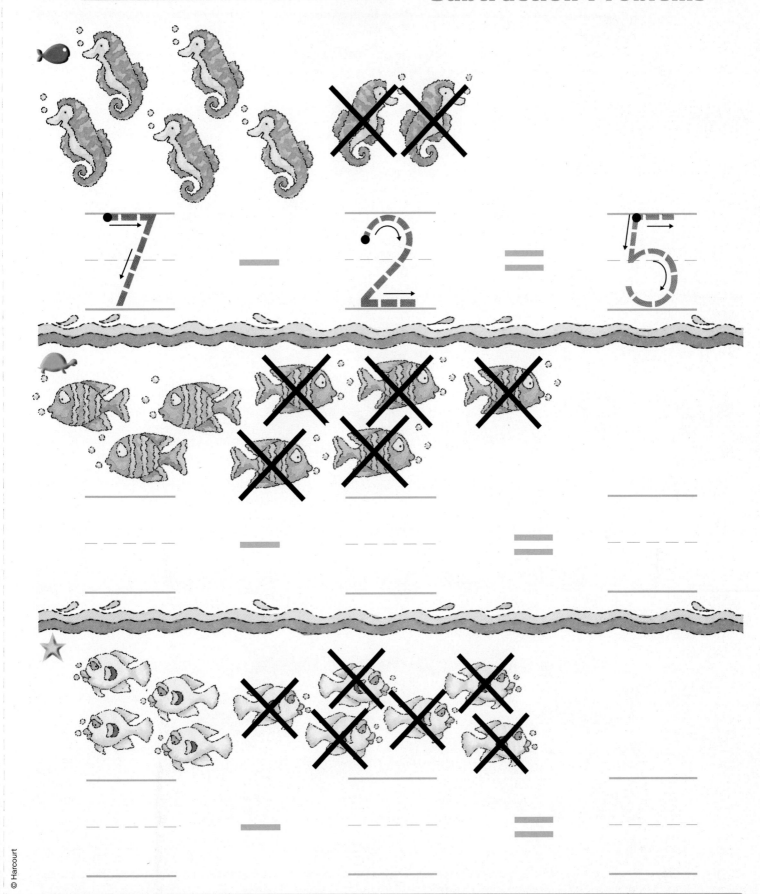

$$7 - 2 = 5$$

🐟 🐋 ⭐ **Tell the subtraction story. Then complete the subtraction sentence.**

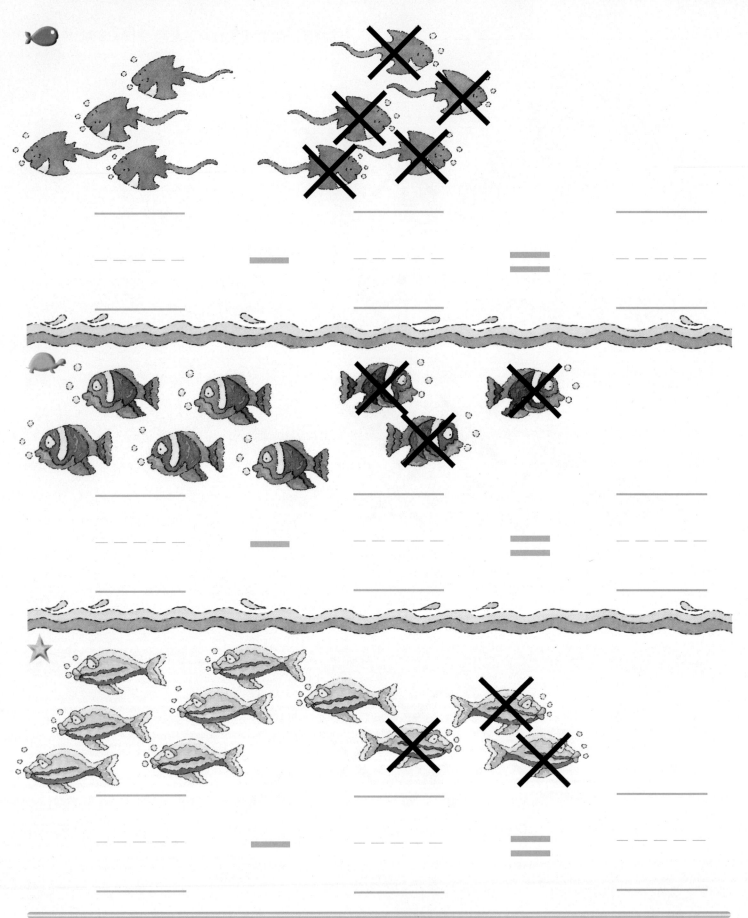

_____ _____ _____

_ _ _ _   ▬   _ _ _ _   ▬▬   _ _ _ _

_____ _____ _____

_____ _____ _____

_ _ _ _   ▬   _ _ _ _   ▬▬   _ _ _ _

_____ _____ _____

_____ _____ _____

_ _ _ _   ▬   _ _ _ _   ▬▬   _ _ _ _

_____ _____ _____

Tell the subtraction story. Then complete the subtraction sentence.

HOME ACTIVITY • Have your child use objects to model the subtraction sentences on this page.

© Harcourt

$$3 - 1 = 2$$

Tell a subtraction story. Act out your story with objects. Draw the objects, and mark an X on the ones you subtract. Complete the subtraction sentence.

_____ _____ _____ _____
_____ − _____ _____ = _____

_____ _____ _____ _____
_____ − _____ _____ = _____

Tell a subtraction story. Act out your story with objects. Draw the objects, and mark an X on the ones you subtract. Complete the subtraction sentence.

HOME ACTIVITY • Tell your child a short subtraction story, and have him or her draw a picture for it.

$$6 + 4 = 10 \qquad \boxed{6 - 4 = 2}$$

$$3 + 2 = 5 \qquad 3 - 2 = 1$$

$$6 + 2 = 8 \qquad 6 - 2 = 4$$

Tell a story about the picture. Circle the number
sentence that tells what is happening in the picture.

© Harcourt

PROBLEM SOLVING

$$5 + 5 = 10 \qquad 5 - 5 = 0$$

$$9 + 1 = 10 \qquad 9 - 1 = 8$$

$$7 + 2 = 9 \qquad 7 - 2 = 5$$

Tell a story about the picture. Circle the number sentence that tells what is happening in the picture.

HOME ACTIVITY • Ask your child to tell you why he or she chose addition or subtraction for each problem.

316

How Many Are Left?

By _____

⬠ **HOME ACTIVITY** • This book will help review subtraction. Invite your child to share this book with you.

1

_____

_____

How many are left? _____

3

5 balloons

4 balloons